Introduction

Customs

Residence and
Permanent Settlement

Real Estate

Taxation

Pension

Health Insurance

Matrimonial Property Law
and Inheritance Law

Education

Citizenship

Edited by Dr. Juerg Steffen

Relocation to Switzerland

An Introduction for High Net Worth Individuals and Entrepreneurs

3rd Edition • Revised and Expanded

IDEOS

ZURICH • LONDON • HONG KONG • NEW YORK

Published by Ideos Publications Ltd. in Zurich.

For general information on our other products and services please visit: *ideospublications.com*

All books published by Ideos Publications are also available as eBooks.

The CIP Catalog record for this book is available from the British Library.

ISBN (Hardback): 978-3-9523859-7-5

ISBN (eBook): 978-3-9524742-7-3

Data correct as at 1 January 2018

Contents

Preface

Dr. Juerg Steffen, Chief Operating Officer, Henley & Partners

Interest in Switzerland as a place of residence has been growing in recent years. Currently, about a quarter of the population in Switzerland is non-Swiss. This is a reversal of the trend in the 19th century, when many people emigrated from Switzerland. Why are we witnessing this shift? Switzerland is a country that is well known for its relatively low taxes, however, this is only a small part of the story since other European countries have equally attractive tax options.

As a Swiss national I may be naturally biased towards my homeland but there are many objectively measurable attributes that set Switzerland apart. Switzerland maintains a level of direct democracy that is unrivaled in the world. It consistently ranks in the top three in many global indexes owing to its high levels of: competitiveness, innovation, human development, and press freedom. It has the longest record of policy neutrality of any country in the world (not participating in any war since 1815). The list goes on.

In my experience one's motivations for changing residence are manifold and it is difficult to make generalizations about them. Being a country with a steady currency, stable democracy, excellent quality of life, and world-class schools and universities, Switzerland has all the right conditions to attract foreign individuals and companies. Ultimately, everyone has his/her own, highly individual, complex mix of reasons for relocating. Relocation should not be taken lightly and should definitely not be a spur-of-the-moment decision.

During my time as a banker and then as a consultant, I realized that many people who want to change their domicile have a tough time navigating all the complexities that a relocation entails. Issues related to healthcare, the schooling system, inheritance taxes, registration formalities, bank secrecy, etc., are all aspects that should be considered before making such an important move.

This book was compiled to help readers who are considering relocating to Switzerland to make an informed and balanced decision. While the book touches on many topics, it is still advisable to consult professional firms (lawyers or consultants) in order to dive deeper into the details of each individual situation.

I would like to thank all the people that contributed to making this second, improved version of the book such a success. In particular, my thanks go out to the authors, without whom this book would not have been possible. They are true experts in their fields, and I am grateful for their theoretical but also practical approach to the challenging topics they cover in their respective chapters. I would also like to thank the publishers and my office for their hard work in making this book a reality.

I hope you, dear reader, will find this third edition informative and enlightening. I would be glad to hear from you regarding any questions or comments you may have.

Dr. Juerg Steffen
Vienna
1 February 2018

1 Introduction to Cross-border Relocation

Dr. Christian H. Kälin, Henley & Partners

Progressing globalization, and the integration of Europe in particular, has had a significant impact on the mobility of many citizens. Many aspects of life are no longer confined to one's home country, but extend worldwide, across borders. Modern careers often inherently require travel, and many companies prefer employees who are internationally mobile. Similarly, financially independent persons are increasingly considering changing their place of residence internationally; the integration of Europe makes this much easier.

With the course of European integration, political stability not only facilitates relocation within Europe, but also contributes to the development of infrastructure, such as improved transport and communication facilities, increased cross-border activities, and the acquisition of property abroad. Overseas property is often purchased as a second home, a holiday home, or even as an entirely new residence. The single currency and free movement of persons and capital within Europe have led to increased property purchases by non-residents, especially in southern Europe, where France, Spain, Italy, and Portugal have particularly benefited. Switzerland has always been a popular holiday destination in Europe, as well as being an attractive option for permanent residence, and the latter option is becoming ever more appealing.

1.1 Relocation and international tax planning

For successful international relocation, various aspects should be considered. First and foremost, the residence and immigration regulations of the desired country must be studied carefully before relocation. The EU has simplified the relocation of citizens within Europe and Switzerland. In addition, in many countries the acquisition of property is now possible without restriction for foreigners. An important exception is Switzerland, where — in principle — residential property cannot be acquired by foreign citizens except by those in possession of an individual permit, or if the real estate project has a corresponding special exemption — this is, however, currently true only for Andermatt in Central Switzerland.

It should also be noted that the acquisition of real estate does not affect immigration and residence regulations. In the US, for example, one must obtain a visa should one wish to extend one's stay. The same applies in Switzerland, of course, but EU citizens enjoy the advantage of being entitled to a residence permit.

In contrast to the US, countries such as the Bahamas, Malta, and Monaco, as well as Australia, Croatia, Panama, Portugal, and Cyprus make it easy for the financially independent to relocate if they can prove that they are not employed in the new country. Residence permits for unemployed persons are usually issued as soon as proof of financial means is available; Croatia requires at least EUR 25,000, while countries such as Monaco and Bermuda require EUR 500,000 or more. In addition, a police certificate must be provided. It is important in such cases to ascertain whether proof of adequate accommodation is required at the time of visa application, or whether property acquisition or the renting of accommodation can be organized after receipt of the visa. It is very easy for EU or European Economic Area (EEA) citizens seeking to relocate to Switzerland to do so, since they can rely on the concept of free movement of persons and therefore have a right to residence. These citizens can concentrate on other aspects of their move, such as tax planning, inheritance planning, and property acquisition.

In principle, one should not be considering a change of residence solely for tax purposes; nevertheless, the impact of relocation on taxation should not be overlooked. If one buys a property only as a vacation home and spends only a few weeks of the year there then nothing changes in terms of personal taxation.

By contrast, if one spends several months at the holiday home, the subject of personal taxation becomes relevant. Specifically, individuals who spend more than three months in a country — even without gainful employment — should be concerned with the issue of tax residence. Individuals who spend more than six months in a country are generally considered to be tax resident and therefore must expect unrestricted taxation. If, however, an individual relocates to a country with a mild tax climate as his/her main residence, considerable tax savings are made possible. In uncomplicated tax planning scenarios, relocation to Monaco, the UK, Malta, or Switzerland, for example, can offer such savings.

Migration is, however, often not without consequences. Many high-taxing countries have enacted laws that make the transfer of residence to a milder tax climate unattractive for their citizens. This is done through an 'exit tax'. In Germany, for example, the Foreign Taxation Act applies. Under certain circumstances, unlimited German tax liability may continue despite the transfer of residence to another country. Essentially, full German taxation still applies although taxes paid in the new country of residence may be accounted for. This rule may remain valid for between five and 10 years after the transfer of residence and can be circumvented only with targeted structuring and, most importantly, ceasing regular or long visits to one's home country.

Although bilateral agreements are designed to avoid double taxation, the relevant national tax laws must be scrutinized before relocation to avoid any unpleasant surprises. Particularly relevant are double taxation agreements, now multilateral tax treaties. It may happen, for example, that two states operating under different national laws both classify a taxpayer as a resident and therefore as fully taxable. In principle, for as long as a double tax agreement exists, tax is due where one is tax resident. In this scenario, tax liability applies to the total worldwide income and possibly, as the case may be, to the net wealth. The second state is referred to as the source country and has the right to tax only the assets located in, or income generated in, that country.

In addition, there are some exact rules — assignment or tie-breaker rules — relating to double or multilateral tax scenarios. For example, if one has a fixed place of residence in two countries, one must indicate the country that is one's main place of residence. If this cannot be easily determined, it is necessary to establish the habitual place of residence or, finally, a decision may be taken based on nationality.

If the jurisdiction is still not established because of dual citizenship, the matter must be clarified between the two states through a mutual agreement procedure.

Tax treaties can often present an advantage for the taxpayer. An example would be if one wanted to leave the old state of residence swiftly because of tax reasons. Here, Switzerland is an interesting example because it has a relatively good network of double taxation agreements. However, these agreements have the restriction that foreigners are taxed at a flat rate. For this reason, it is sometimes better to move to Switzerland and be taxed as normal than to use the flat tax rate. Nonetheless, where possible it is better to obtain a tax ruling before taking up tax residence in another country.

By contrast, one is less protected if one takes up residence in a state that does not have a tax treaty with one's former state of residence, for example, when emigrating from Germany to Monaco. As no tax treaty applies between these two states, taxpayers find it difficult to end tax residence in the old country of residence. Often, the only way to avoid being be taxed by high-taxing countries from which one has relocated is by taking the radical step of cutting all connections to one's country of origin. This applies particularly to Germany, but also to many other high-taxing countries.

The Standard for Automatic Exchange of Financial Account Information, introduced by the Organisation for Economic Co-operation and Development (OECD), outlines automatic exchange of financial account information between countries through a set of rules detailed in the Common Reporting Standard (CRS). The CRS requires financial institutions to report account holder information to local tax authorities who, in turn, automatically exchange that information on an annual basis with the tax authorities where these account holders are tax resident. The first phase of the CRS was initiated in 2017 and is in the process of coming into force in almost every significant economy except the US.

With the introduction of the CRS, alternative residence or citizenship — and the fiscal and security benefits associated with them — is being taken more seriously by those wanting to operate globally, reduce their exposure to external threats, increase their international flexibility, and explore new opportunities.

The CRS has been widely welcomed as a positive, globally coordinated move towards greater financial transparency and accountability. Rightly or wrongly, however, some wealthy individuals and families who reside in developing countries fear that the necessary regulations and safeguards taken to protect privacy may not be sufficiently effective, thereby making personal and financial information available to criminal elements and threatening their safety and security. Concerned individuals may look into relocating and becoming tax resident in a country where the vital controls and regulations around cross-border sharing of information are in place. Switzerland is particularly safe in this regard and, for this reason, will be in the coming years of increasing interest to wealthy families as a secure place of residence.

1.2 Estate planning and inheritance tax

Inheritance law, inheritance tax, and the corresponding estate planning and inheritance tax planning are closely intertwined with the topic of tax planning. Inheritance and gift taxes depend on the last place of residence of the deceased or benefactor, but where the heirs or beneficiaries are located or which citizenship they hold can also be relevant. Germany, specifically, is the only country in which inheritance tax must be paid by the heir if he/she is tax resident in Germany. Tax relief in the case of inheritance is therefore possible only if both the deceased and the heir are not resident in Germany. In the US, it is relevant if anyone concerned has US citizenship. Applicable inheritance law as well as possible inheritance and gift taxes can have both positive and negative effects on a change of residence, depending on the country of residence. Some countries permit other asset dispositions because of death, for example, the right to a compulsory share, greater freedom of testament, or reversed, stricter, forced heirship rules.

Thorough estate planning is particularly recommended in the context of international relocation. It is useful to consult experts in the present country of residence as well as in the destination country. In addition, the corresponding structuring of real estate, wherever located, should be factored in.

If the appeal of a reasonable tax climate induces relocation, Switzerland is a sensible consideration. Migration is often the only way to legally reduce the tax burden in high-taxing countries; nevertheless, one shouldn't seek to relocate solely for tax reasons. If a second home already exists, the decision is somewhat simpler since one is familiar with many of the usual areas of uncertainty, for example, quality of life or real estate options.

1.3 Acquisition and structuring of real estate

Many real estate purchases are entered into despite the buyers not having the necessary knowledge about tax and/or other implications. In the case of a relocation, not only should the climate and the living conditions in one's new home country be considered, but also that some practices are different from those in one's former home country. The proverb 'different countries, different customs' should not be disregarded — one should be particularly aware that different legal regulations apply in the case of transfer of residence, particularly in the fields of property and tax law. It is therefore critical when planning relocation to consider not only the local justice system, but also the laws and regulations of the destination country, for which one should obtain detailed information and adapt or plan accordingly. In any event, in most countries one must comply with certain basic rules in order to secure property acquisitions. In this respect Switzerland is exemplary, since land purchases can typically be handled safely and without any problems.

In the case of relocation and associated private property purchase, the main objective should be an improved quality of life. It is often the case, however, particularly in cases of cross-border relocation that not all potential problems are considered, which is why it is important to seek professional counsel from lawyers, tax experts, architects, and reputable real estate companies. Ideally, each expert should not only be knowledgeable about the local conditions but also have experience in advising on relocation to the destination country. The resulting additional costs are compensated for in most instances by a fast and impeccable structuring and execution of the purchase.

In addition, the acquisition of real estate is always a capital investment; conservation of value and value growth, as well as tax and inheritance aspects, are therefore important factors to consider. Before acquiring a property, it is important to clarify these essential basic conditions to ensure protection from unexpected legal and tax consequences. While this applies to real estate in general, it is particularly relevant to foreign real estate.

A major advantage of moving to Switzerland is that there is no language barrier for German-, French- or Italian-speaking buyers, minimizing the potential for misunderstandings during the purchase of real estate. In most cases, this is not an obstacle, but it is certainly a relief for many buyers who plan to move to Switzerland.

When selecting a property, not only do the local legal and tax factors play a role; one should also investigate the development plans for the immediate surroundings. This is particularly important in a new country with which at first one is not as well acquainted as one's former homeland. For example, a beautiful property can quickly become unattractive if a highway is built nearby, or if a neighbor's construction project limits or even blocks an idyllic view. Major projects for which one should keep an eye out include the construction of future highways, airport extensions, high voltage lines, and landfills, because all these can affect one's quality of life and the value of one's property. Further considerations that would affect the price level at the time of purchase and in the future are site quality and infrastructure. One should ask oneself, for example, Where is the property located: is it on a quiet, peaceful street? What is the quality of the surrounding infrastructure? What is the distance to the nearest school, doctor, or hospital, and to basic amenities such as a post office, bank, and shops? How accessible is the connection to national roads and highways? What is the journey time to the nearest airport? How well developed is the public transport system?

1.4 International insurance

Various aspects of insurance must be understood when planning international relocation, the most notable being health insurance. All too often, health insurance is not prudently factored in or included in advice to internationally mobile clients, which is possibly the reason there are relatively few companies worldwide that can truly and independently advise on this sensitive but important topic.

Finding good health insurance is not as simple as one might think, making it all the more important to identify a reliable insurer when relocating to ensure that, in the event of illness or an accident abroad, insurance cover is adequate and readily available. When considering providers and their offerings, try to identify which insurer places the fewest restrictions on one's choice of doctors and/or hospitals. Those who live, work, run a company, or retire abroad should be covered as widely as possible, ideally globally.

If a stay in a foreign European country is temporary, one can rely on the emergency care of basic state insurance for at least minimum coverage. In addition, travel insurance can be obtained for illness and accident cover with almost every local healthcare provider. In the case of a definitive residence insurance, however, it is advisable to be thoroughly informed about local insurance. As soon as the relocation process is officially completed, ensure that the planning and implementation of the changes to one's health insurance plan are also completed. Otherwise one risks not only being limited to consulting free doctors and hospitals, but in a worst case scenario, having temporarily no insurance cover at all.

For international relocation, other insurance policies should be considered too, however, since these are usually free of the restrictions found in health insurance they can, and often should, be completed or changed after the relocation. While the best deals are often concluded on the spot, it is important to assess whether the cover applies abroad as well. For example, a policy may cease to provide cover upon migration, or there may be a geographic restriction for a motor vehicle insurance. Confirmation that insurance cover will still exist ought to be obtained in writing so that, in the event of a possible damage claim, cover can be proved beyond doubt. One is usually well advised to select an internationally active insurance company, particularly for the insurance of special valuables such as art or jewelry. Insurance coverage is in many instances applicable worldwide and can be maintained even in the event of subsequent migration, such as in the case of an international health insurance policy.

1.5 Financial planning

Last but not least, pension and financial planning need to be re-parameterized during international relocation. As tax and legal framework conditions change during relocation, so should financial planning be adapted to the new situation.

For relocation purposes, financial planning starts with the reference currency, which often changes when one migrates across borders. If, for example, one moves from the US to Switzerland, the new reference currency is no longer the US dollar but the Swiss franc. The re-evaluation of financial assets in the relevant currency is best planned and implemented with a qualified investment manager. This is less relevant in the case of relocation within the Eurozone, but here too, a different currency weighting may make sense because time spent traveling may increase. Asset and pension planning can therefore be improved.

Often, capital that is tied up in pension funds regulated in state-regulated systems can be dissolved. The reallocation or liquidation of one's retirement provisions such as pension claims, life insurance, or pension funds is worth considering, since this can lead to tax breaks, particularly in the country of migration, and have a positive effect on liquidity planning. This may in some circumstances need to be adjusted for the new place of residence since expenditure may increase or decrease. Furthermore, it may be sensible or necessary to 'buy into' the pension system of the new country of residence, and this may be advantageous from a tax perspective. In all events, these points should be very carefully checked.

It is very important to include estate planning and inheritance structures (for example, partnerships, foundations, trusts, and family holding companies) in financial planning for relocation. For example, a migrant setting up home in Malta, the UK, Ireland, St. Kitts and Nevis, or the Bahamas can structure assets in such a way that the appointment of a freely selectable successor is made possible. This is only rarely the case in countries such as Switzerland or others that follow a civil law tradition that includes forced heirship. Asset protection is also a significant factor in relocation and this is an especially important topic in the US. The American legal system facilitates civil lawsuits to such an extent that it makes sense to protect one's assets or part thereof, such as property ownership, from vulnerability by setting up appropriate structures. Correspondingly designed asset protection trusts, as well as specifically structured life insurance policies, are particularly suitable for this purpose. Even though this problem applies mainly in the US, it is becoming increasingly an issue in Europe and thereby putting European assets at risk.

International relocation should for all these reasons be planned carefully and accompanied by professional support to best position oneself to take advantage of all the positive aspects of relocation. As this introduction shows, many details must be considered, clarified and checked. One should review not only tax advantages or disadvantages, but also factors such as legislation, financial and estate planning, and asset protection. Finally, it is important that one is aware that in the acquisition of real estate there is potential for growth in value. Relocation is not only an opportunity to enjoy an international lifestyle and all potential tax advantages, it also presents the possibility of optimizing personal wealth and providing for oneself and one's family in an international dimension. Switzerland offers optimal conditions in this regard.

About the author

DR. CHRISTIAN H. KÄLIN, TEP, IMCM, Chairman of Henley & Partners, is considered one of the world's foremost experts in investment migration and citizenship-by-investment, a field he pioneered. Holding master's and PhD degrees in law from the University of Zurich, he is a sought-after speaker and advises governments and international organizations. He is the author, co-author, or editor of many publications, including standard works such as the *Global Residence and Citizenship Handbook*, the *Henley & Partners – Kochenov Quality of Nationality Index*, and the *Switzerland Business & Investment Handbook*.

2 Customs in Switzerland

Marc Buchmann, Fischer Ramp Partner

As a general rule, individuals relocating to Switzerland may import the contents of their household, personal collections, animals, and vehicles duty free, provided the imported goods have been in the individual's personal use for at least six months prior to immigration, and the individual continues using the items after relocation in Switzerland.

Vehicles imported during the course of immigration have to pass a technical inspection within one year after their import. A Swiss driving license should also be obtained. Those who hold foreign driving licenses are in most cases not required to take a driving test. Only holders of driving licenses from a few states are required to pass both a theoretical exam and a practical driving examination.

2.1 Customs treatment of household items

Individuals relocating to Switzerland may import their household items duty free, provided the items have been in use at least six months prior to immigration and continues to be used after residence is taken up. The definition of household items is fairly broad and depends on a variety of factors and on the individual's circumstances.

Household inventories and, for example, standard tobacco products of an accepted quantity may also be imported duty free. Restrictions apply with regard to alcoholic beverages (less than 25% alcoholic content, not exceeding 200 liters, more than 25% alcoholic content, not exceeding 12 liters).

2.2 Procedure

At the time of importing household items, immigrating individuals are required to submit the following documents to the customs office:

- Application form 18.44 (see *ezv.admin.ch*, > Information individuals > Personal property, students, holiday homes, getting married and inheritance > Importing into Switzerland)
- A list indicating all goods to be imported. If goods are to be declared for customs purposes, they have to be listed separately at the end of the document
- Individuals from non-EU or non-EFTA countries have to provide proof of a residence permit. Individuals from EU and from EFTA countries do not have to provide confirmation of a residence permit. However, proof of transfer of domicile has to be demonstrated in another way (for example, with a lease agreement, employment agreement, or a confirmation from the country of departure)
- In the case of importing a vehicle, a registration certificate issued by the foreign authority is required

The customs office may request additional documents in order to verify eligibility for duty-free importation.

If a carrier is in charge of importing the household items, the documents listed above need to be provided to the carrier.

Importation of household items can only take place during official working hours (Monday to Friday, see *ezv.admin.ch*, Swiss Customs Administration > The FCA > Organization > Border crossings and customs offices, opening hours).

2.3 Importation timeframe

Household items have to be imported at the time of immigration, within a two-year period following immigration at the latest. The main prerequisite for duty-free importation is that the items have been in use for a period of at least six months before the date of immigration. In case of goods imported at a later stage, duty exemption will be granted only under certain conditions.

2.4 Importation of vehicles

Vehicles can be imported duty free, provided the vehicles have been used six months prior to immigration. The importation of the vehicle must be declared separately. The vehicle's license number and category have to be indicated in the declaration. If the importation requires a technical inspection, the customs authority will provide form 13.20A.

Duties on vehicles

If the vehicle has been used for a period of less than six months prior to importation, the duty exemption does not apply and the vehicle is subject to duties. The vehicle owner needs to declare the vehicle to customs and the applicant needs to file the following documents:

- The vehicle's invoice or purchase agreement
- Vehicle license
- Passport or identification document (ID)
- Document confirming the origin of the vehicle, if available

In the event of a non-duty-free importation of a vehicle, the following contributions and taxes will be levied:

- Car tax of 4% levied on the value of the vehicle, including customs duties
- VAT of 8% on the value of the vehicle, including customs duties and vehicle tax
- Customs duties (approximately CHF 12 up to CHF 15 per 100 kilograms depending on the weight or capacity of the vehicle)
- An administration fee

Vehicles can be imported duty free provided a free-trade treaty exists between Switzerland and the country of origin, for example, EU/EFTA countries.

If the vehicle will only be used in Switzerland temporarily, permission may be requested allowing the use of the vehicle for a period of two years without declaring it to customs.[1] After the two-year period, the vehicle must be exported or has to be declared to customs.

1 Form 15.30

Vehicle authorization

Vehicles that are imported in the course of relocation need to be authorized within one year of immigration. The vehicle owner is required to arrange a date for the technical inspection.

Prior to inspection, the vehicle owner has to provide the following documents to the traffic authorities:

- Registration certificate
- Manual indicating the maximum speed, capacity, performance, etc.
- Form 13.20A (the form is provided if the vehicle was imported at the time of immigration and declared as a household item)
- Car insurance statement
- Certificate of conformity in accordance with EU regulations, if available
- Emission test certificate
- Form 18.44

Depending on the origin of the vehicle, it may be sensible to have an expert examine the vehicle prior to technical inspection, to establish whether adjustments are required to comply with Swiss regulations.

Issuance of a Swiss driving license

Foreign driving licenses must be exchanged for a Swiss license within a three- or 12-month period, depending on the country of origin of the driving license. After 12 months, the license holder is not entitled to use the foreign license anymore.

In order to exchange the foreign driving license for a Swiss license, the following documents have to be filed with the Swiss traffic authority:

- Application form
- Foreign driving license (original required)
- Residence permit
- Color photograph (format 35 mm × 45 mm)
- Results of eye inspection

If the driving license holder is from a non-EU/EFTA country or other countries such as Israel, Canada etc.,[2] the applicant is required to pass a driver's test within three months following the relocation.

---

2 Other exempt driving licenses are those originating from Andorra, Australia, Canada, Israel, Japan, Monaco, Morocco, New Zealand, San Marino, Singapore, South Korea, Taiwan, Tunisia, and the US

Driver's inspection and theoretical exam

During the driver's inspection, an official examiner will assess the license holder's driving skills and knowledge of national traffic rules.

The applicant must bring the foreign driving license, a vehicle and residence permit to the driver's inspection.

If the applicant does not pass the inspection, he/she is requested to prepare and pass the Swiss driving test which consists of a theoretical and practical exam. These exams require preparation and driving lessons with an instructor.

Individuals using vehicles for professional purposes (for example, lorry or taxi drivers) may need to pass an additional theoretical exam. EU/EFTA driving license holders are exempt from the theoretical exam.

When relocating to Switzerland it is important to understand the regulations that apply when importing goods from the country of origin. In general, most items can be imported duty free, provided that the items have been in use for six months prior to relocation and continue to be used after immigration.

Links to useful online resources

The following web pages may be helpful when one is preparing to relocate to Switzerland:

- *ezv.admin.ch*
  Provides relevant information related to the customs procedure and forms to prepare and file
- *ch.ch*
  Provides an overview of important Swiss topics related to official requirements

About the author

MARC BUCHMANN, attorney and Swiss-qualified tax expert, is a senior associate at Fischer Ramp Partner. He advises private clients on national and international tax aspects and corporates on tax planning matters. He also acts in tax litigations. Marc Buchmann publishes articles in tax law journals and lectures at the Swiss Institute of Tax Law (SIST).

Fischer Ramp Partner is a private-client, boutique law firm specializing in tax and private client-related matters (*frp-law.ch*).

3 Residence Permits and Permanent Settlement

Thomas Stoltz, Bär & Karrer AG

The motivations to live and work in Switzerland are manifold. The high income level, economic and political stability, low tax burden, and a well-developed education system are just a few such motivations. Persons who intend to live, pursue employment in, or take their families to Switzerland, must inevitably deal with the applicable legal provisions regarding foreign nationals.

Swiss legislation and international regulations form the legal basis for controlling the entry and exit of foreigners, and define the prerequisites of their stay. Switzerland has enacted specific laws and has entered into different agreements with other countries to regulate the laws on foreign nationals.

This chapter provides a brief introduction to entry and residence requirements for foreigners in Switzerland. It also delves into the different legal aspects, the various types of residence and work permits, including their particular prerequisites, and family reunification.

3.1 Legal basis

Switzerland regulates the entry and residence of foreigners in two ways. In the case of EU/EFTA citizens, the Agreement on the Free Movement of Persons (AFMP)[1] of 21 June 1999 between the EU and its member states, and the Swiss Confederation, applies. In the case of non-EU/EFTA citizens, the Federal Act on

1 SR 0.142.112.681

Foreign Nationals (FNA)[2] applies, as well as another important legislative text, the Ordinance of 24 October 2007 on Admission, Period of Stay and Employment (ASEO).[3]

For citizens of EU member states, their family members, and certain service providers from these states, the AFMP provides comprehensive regulations for the reciprocal movement of persons between states. The FNA is therefore only applicable to EU/EFTA citizens if the AFMP and its implementing provisions do not contain any divergent provisions, or if the regulations of the FNA are more favorable for citizens and their family members.[4] The FNA regulates the admission of foreign nationals and aims to improve the legal status and integration of foreign nationals in Switzerland. It also protects the *ordre public.*

3.2 Differences between the FNA and the AFMP

The dual system (the AFMP and FNA) creates a privileged status for EU/EFTA nationals in terms of access to the Swiss labor market. To third-country nationals, however, restrictive authorization that lays down high entry hurdles applies. The AFMP and FNA differ in some aspects:[5]

- The AFMP grants a legal right of entry, residence, access to work as an employed person, establishment on a self-employed basis, and the right to stay in Switzerland. It does not leave the decision up to the discretion of local authorities
- The FNA on the other hand, grants the executive authorities a wide margin of discretion. The authorities may decide whether or not they issue a permit. Art 96 of the FNA regulates the exercise of discretion in that it stipulates that authorities shall take into account public interest and personal circumstances, as well as the degree of integration of foreign nationals[6]
- One of the fundamental principles of the AFMP is the non-discrimination against nationals who are lawfully resident in the territory of a Contracting Party[7]

There are also differences in legal procedures and the voidability of rulings by authorities. Citizens of EU/EFTA countries may use the ordinary courts. They may, for example, file an appeal in matters of public law at the Federal Supreme Court,

2 SR 142.20
3 SR 142.201
4 art 12 AFMP
5 Factsheet on Free Movement of Persons with the European Union, State Secretariat for Migration (SEM)
6 *Spezialisierungskurs im Arbeitsrecht* 2013/2014, Dr. iur. Felix Klaus, s 4 seq
7 art 2 AFMP and annexes I, II and III

whereas citizens of non-EU/EFTA countries do not have the option to appeal.[8] They do not have any other alternatives to reach the Federal Supreme Court.[9]

3.3 Types of permits

Depending on the nationality of a person, the duration of his/her stay, and whether or not he/she is working, different types of permits with different prerequisites apply.

Residence and work permits

General

There are different types of residence permits in Switzerland. Short-term permits (L-permits) are issued for a certain period of time. The period of validity of the permit is identical to the term of the employment contract. In general, L-permits are valid for 12 months. In exceptional cases, these permits can be extended once to an overall duration of no more than 24 months, provided the holder works for the same employer throughout this time. After that, a long-term work permit is required.

The residence permit (B-permit) is issued for an initial period of one year, and may be renewed. An application for renewal must be filed by the permit holder. The conditions for granting the permit must, in general, be checked each year by the competent authority. In practice, the renewal of B-permits is a formality, unless there are reasons against a renewal, such as criminal offences, dependence on social security, or major changes in the labor market. There is, however, no statutory right to the renewal of the permit.

Foreign nationals who have stayed in Switzerland for a certain period of time may apply for an unlimited residence permit (C-permit). The required period of stay is generally 10 years. Depending on the nationality of foreigners, a different minimum period may apply.[10]

EU/EFTA citizens

Citizens of the EU/EFTA have a legal entitlement to a work- and residence permit if an employment contract with a company in Switzerland has been issued. There are no restrictions on granting permits. Depending on the (expected) duration of the contract, different permits apply.

---

8 art 83 let C Federal Act of 17 June 2005 on the Federal Supreme Court, SR 173.110

9 *Spezialisierungskurs im Arbeitsrecht* 2013/2014, Dr. iur. Felix Klaus, s 8 seq

10 Factsheet on Residing in Switzerland and taking up gainful activity, State Secretariat for Migration (SEM)

Nationals of EU/EFTA member states do not need a work permit if they work for less than 90 days per calendar year for a company in Switzerland. However, registration is required if employment is for more than eight days per calendar year. This registration can be done online. It is important to note that the registration needs to be filed at least eight days before employment commences in Switzerland. Usually, the following documents and information have to be submitted:

- Copy of passport
- Name and address of the employer in Switzerland
- Job title and project in Switzerland
- Employment start and end dates
- Work days

If the gainful activities continue for longer than 90 days per calendar year, a specific work permit is required.

EU/EFTA citizens may claim one of the following work and residence permits for a gainful activity that exceeds three months:

- A short-term residence and work permit, issued for employment between three months and 364 days (L-permit)
- A residence and work permit for employment of more than 12 months (B-permit)
- The unlimited residence permit (C-permit), issued to EU-17/EFTA citizens after five years' regular and uninterrupted residence in Switzerland, pursuant to settlement treaties or reciprocal agreements (except of Cyprus and Malta, as the AFMP does not contain any provisions relating to these countries). The required period of stay for a C-permit is five or 10 years.[11] There is no legal right to an unlimited residence permit (C-permit)[12]

EU/EFTA citizens who want to work on a self-employed basis have to submit an application together with a business plan, proof of financial means, and a certificate of registration. Such a permit has to be obtained from the labor market authorities of the canton in which the work will be provided. Furthermore, Swiss authorities are allowed to request this proof at any time, even after the permit has been issued, if there are serious doubts regarding the financial situation of the self-employed foreigner.

---

11 art 34 FNA

12 'Residence permits for EU/EFTA nationals' *(State Secretariat for Migration — SEM) sem.admin.ch/sem/en/home/themen/aufenthalt/eu_efta.html* accessed 28 July 2017

Non-EU/EFTA citizens

Work permits for citizens of non-EU/EFTA countries are subject to a nation-wide quota. The annual quota is set by the Swiss Confederation and cantons, that take into account the macroeconomic interests and the current labor market. The issuance of work permits also depends on whether the conditions of work and salary are equal to Swiss standards. Additional payments can be required to match Swiss standards. This provision protects domestic employees from wage dumping and abusive working conditions. In addition, employees from non-EU/EFTA countries are only permitted to the Swiss labor market if no appropriate candidate can be found throughout Switzerland and other EU/EFTA countries. The foreign employee must be considered to be especially qualified for the position in question. The authorities will require proof that an employer made an effort to recruit in Switzerland and EU/EFTA countries, and that no qualified Swiss citizen, foreign national with a Swiss residence permit, or EU/EFTA citizen could be found. Candidates are also required to fulfill personal requirements according to the FNA.[13]

Depending on the purpose of the stay, different types of permits apply. The short-term residence permit (L-permit) will allow the stay and gainful activity within Switzerland for 12 months. Due to the priority of Swiss citizens and nationals of EU/EFTA states in the labor market and the quota requirement, it is difficult to obtain such a permit. The Residence permit (B-permit) is for persons who are expected to stay and work in Switzerland for more than 12 months. Since the quota for B-permits is smaller than for L-permits, obtaining a B-permit is even more difficult. In matters of the unlimited residence permit (C-permit), the same rules apply as for EU/EFTA citizens.[14]

A non-EU/EFTA citizen who intends to be self-employed must submit an application together with a business plan, proof of financial means, and a certificate of registration. The competent authority will review the business plan and assess the relevant market situation.

Residence permit without employment

Every EU/EFTA citizen who is not gainfully employed has the right to stay in Switzerland (with his/her family) if he/she has sufficient financial resources to make a living. This is the case if he/she is not in need of social welfare. Pensioners are only required to prove that the available financial resources exceed the amount that would

13 art 23 and 24 FNA

14 art 23 f FNA; 'Residence permits for EU/EFTA nationals', *(State Secretariat for Migration — SEM), sem.admin.ch/sem/en/home/themen/aufenthalt/nicht_eu_efta.html* accessed 28 July 2017

qualify them to obtain supplementary benefits (according to the AHVG). In addition, all of the applicants must take out health- and accident-insurance, covering all risks.[15]

Citizens of non-EU/EFTA countries do not require a permit for any period of stay without gainful employment of up to three months; if the visa indicates a shorter period of stay this period applies.[16] A permit is required for foreign nationals intending to stay for longer than three months without entering into employment.[17] Pensioners of non-EU/EFTA countries may be admitted if they have reached a minimum age of 55 years, have special personal relations to Switzerland, and have the required financial means.[18] In order to prove a special personal relationship with Switzerland, an applicant would need to show, for example, previous longer stays in Switzerland (such as holidays, education, or employment), intensive business and personal connections to Switzerland, or the presence of close relatives (for example, parents or children). The FNA stipulates the necessary financial resources.[19] Applicants must have sufficient resources (pensions, assets) to take care of themselves and their families so that the risk of welfare dependency is assessed to be negligibly small.[20]

3.4 Cross-border services

EU/EFTA citizens who intend to provide services in Switzerland may enter and stay in Switzerland for a maximum of 90 effective working days per calendar year without any permit. This applies to self-employed occupation for a limited time without settlement in Switzerland, as well as to employees of firms based in the EU who are sent to Switzerland to provide a service. If a special bilateral agreement is applicable to the provided service the person may stay in Switzerland for as long as the service is being carried out.[21] The AFMP does not include full freedom to provide cross-border services, as is possible within the EU. The provision of financial services in Switzerland (where a license and supervision are required) and the provision of services regarding job placement and staff leasing services (by legal entities based in an EU/EFTA member state) have not been liberalized.[22]

15 Factsheet on Residing in Switzerland without gainful activity, State Secretariat for Migration (SEM)
16 art 10 para 1 FNA
17 art 10 para 2 FNA
18 art 28 FNA
19 art 28 para 1 let c FNA
20 *Weisungen und Erläuterungen Ausländerbereich (Weisungen AuG)*, p 199 seq, 2013, State Secretariat for Migration (SEM)
21 art 5 para 1 AFMP
22 Factsheet on Cross-border service provision (EU/EFTA), State Secretariat for Migration (SEM); *Weisungen VEP, Wesiungen und Erläuterungen zur Verordnung über die Einführung des freien Personenverkehrs*, p 86 seq, 2017, State Secretariat for Migration (SEM)

Service providers are required to register their services of more than eight days per calendar year online. The registration must take place eight days in advance. However, service providers in so-called risk industries (building sector, hotel and restaurant industry, security services, etc.) must register from the first day onwards. Switzerland regulates service providers with the *Entsendegesetz* and the relevant regulations.[23]

Non-EU/EFTA citizens who provide cross-border services or who are employed in Switzerland on behalf of a foreign employer require a permit if the activity lasts longer than eight days within a calendar year.[24] Service providers of certain industries require a permit, irrespective of the duration of their activity.[25] Non-EU/EFTA citizens who are granted a permit to work or to provide services in Switzerland for up to four months during one calendar year do not need to register.[26]

Cross-border commuters

The cross-border permit (G-permit) is for cross-border commuters who are nationals of EU/EFTA member states, reside in an EU/EFTA member state, and work in Switzerland. They are granted occupational and geographical mobility within Switzerland, irrespective of whether or not they are working in an employed or self-employed capacity. Cross-border commuters must return to their main place of residence outside of Switzerland at least once a week. Transitional conditions (border zones and restrictions concerning the Swiss labor market) apply to Croatian cross-border commuters.[27]

Non-EU/EFTA cross-border commuters are people with a permanent right of residence in a neighbouring state, who have resided in the neighbouring border zone for at least six months, and work within Switzerland.[28] Cross-border commuters must return to their main place of residence outside of Switzerland at least once a week.[29] If cross-border commuters want to change jobs or occupations, they need permission. Furthermore, the labor market requirement (especially regarding precedence given to the domestic workforce)[30] must be fulfilled.[31]

23 SR 823.20 and SR 823.201
24 art 14 para 1 ASEO
25 art 14 para 3 ASEO
26 art 12 para 1 ASEO; *Weisungen und Erläuterungen Ausländerbereich (Weisungen AuG)*, p 174 seq, 2013, State Secretariat for Migration (SEM)
27 Factsheet on Cross-border commuters, State Secretariat for Migration (SEM)
28 art 25 para 1 FNA
29 art 35 para 2 FNA
30 art 21 FNA
31 art 17 of the AFMP appendix I; 'Cross-border commuters (G-permit)', *Office for Economy and Labour, awa.zh.ch/internet/volkswirtschaftsdirektion/awa/en/arbeitsbewilligungen/drittstaaten/grenzgaenger.html#subtitle-content-internet-volkswirtschaftsdirektion-awa-en-arbeitsbewilligungen-drittstaaten-grenzgaenger-jcr-content-contentPar-textimage_0* accessed 28 July 2017

3.5 Family reunification (*Familiennachzug*)

The purpose of family reunification is to enable families to live together legally and securely. Before granting family reunification it must therefore be clarified where the actual center of family life is. If it remains abroad, the conditions of family reunification are not met.[32]

EU/EFTA nationals

Citizens of EU/EFTA countries who have been granted the right to stay in Switzerland may extend this right to certain family members.[33] They may bring their spouse and their own children or their spouse's children, who are under the age of 21 or receive support. They may also bring their own parents or their spouse's parents, if they receive support. The nationality of these family members is irrelevant. The right of these family members to stay in Switzerland only persists for as long as the right of the original applicant exists.[34] The family members also have the right to access the labor market without restrictions.[35]

Persons wanting to bring their family members to Switzerland must provide proof of adequate accommodation for their family members. This means that the accommodation must reflect typical living conditions of Swiss citizens.

In the case of divorce, family members generally lose the right to stay in Switzerland. This signifies that they have to establish their right to stay by other means, for example, by applying for a residence permit in their own capacity. In the case of non-EU/EFTA citizens, the FNA applies.

In the case of death of the original applicant, family members who were living with this person at the time of his/her death may stay in Switzerland if one of the following conditions are met:

- The person was economically active and held a Swiss residence permit for EU/EFTA citizens for at least two years before he/she died
- The cause of death was either work related or caused by an illness
- The spouse holds Swiss citizenship or lost this citizenship through marriage[36]

There are transitional conditions that apply to Croatian nationals.[37]

32 *Weisungen und Erläuterungen Ausländerbereich (Weisungen AuG)*, p 237, 2013, State Secretariat for Migration (SEM)

33 art 3 para 1 AFMP appendix I

34 art 3 para 4 AFMP appendix I

35 art 3 para 4 AFMP appendix I; Factsheet on Family Reunification, State Secretariat for Migration (SEM)

36 Factsheet on Family Reunification, State Secretariat for Migration (SEM)

37 Factsheet on Croatia: Entry and stays, State Secretariat for Migration (SEM)

Third-country nationals

Family reunification for third-country nationals living in Switzerland (with a C- or a B-permit) is more restricted. Third-country nationals may only bring their spouse and their children (under 18 years of age) with them,[38] and only if they live with the permit holder. The permit holder must have suitable accommodation for all family members (some cantons use the following rule: number of persons minus one equals the minimum number of rooms of accommodation required). Family reunification must be claimed within a certain period of time, generally five years,[39] to support rapid integration. A belated family reunification is only granted if important family reasons are invoked.

The right of a permit holder's spouse and children to be granted residence permits, and to have their residence permits extended, subsists after the dissolution of the marriage or of the family household if (i) the marriage lasted a minimum of three years and integration has been successful; or (ii) important personal reasons make an extended residence in Switzerland necessary (*Härtefall*).[40]

The spouse and children of a Swiss national, or of a person with a residence permit, may work on a salaried or self-employed basis anywhere in Switzerland.[41]

All provisions regarding family reunifications on foreign spouses also apply *mutatis mutandis* to registered partnerships of same-sex couples, in accordance with the Federal Act of 18 June 2004 on the Registered Partnership between Persons of the Same Sex.[42] Many same-sex couples abstain from registering their partnerships, in some cases due to possible disadvantages in their home countries. In such cases, a residence permit may still be granted.[43] The same rule may be applicable regarding cohabitees of Swiss citizens.[44]

Swiss citizens

In the case of foreign family members of Swiss nationals, a distinction applies between those who are already in possession of a permanent residence permit in an EU/EFTA member state, and those who are not.[45]

38 art 43 and 44 FNA
39 art 47 FNA; art 73 ASEO
40 art 50 FNA
41 art 42–44 and art 46 FNA
42 SR 211.231
43 art 31 ASEO; art 30 para 1 let B FNA
44 Weisungen und Erläuterungen Ausländerbereich (Weisungen AuG), p 237 seq, 2013, State Secretariat for Migration (SEM)
45 art 42 para 2 FNA

If the family members of a Swiss national are not in possession of permanent residence permits, the spouse and unmarried children under 18 are entitled to be granted a residence permit.[46] Children under 12 are entitled to be granted a permanent residence permit.[47] The right of family reunification is only granted if the requirement of living together is met.

If the family members are already in possession of permanent residence permits in an EU/EFTA member state, they are entitled to be granted residence permits in Switzerland. Swiss citizens may bring their spouse and relatives in descending line who are under the age of 21 or who receive support and relatives of either spouse in ascending line who receive support.[48] Children under 12 are entitled to be granted a permanent residence permit with no time limit.[49]

The AFMP is only applicable under cross-border circumstances, as in the case of Swiss citizens who are returning from an EU/EFTA member state with their family members. According to the new practice of the Federal Supreme Court, the right of family reunification[50] is no longer limited to family members who hold residence permits in EU/EFTA member states. The Federal Court thus adopted the new jurisprudence of the European Court of Justice.[51]

However, the FNA still requires the family members who are not nationals of EU/EFTA countries, to have residence permits in EU/EFTA member states. This condition has not been changed.[52]

3.6 Swiss Citizenship Act

In addition to residence permits, work permits, and permanent settlement, the Swiss Citizenship Act is important for foreign nationals, as it stipulates the prerequisites for naturalization in Switzerland. The Federal Council has decided to bring a revised Swiss Citizenship Act and the respective regulations into force on 1 January 2018. The new law is set to unify and harmonize naturalization practices across the cantons. The most important innovation of the Act is that a foreign national may now file an application for naturalization after 10 years' residence in

46 art 42 para 1 FNA
47 art 42 para 4 FNA; art 47 FNA
48 art 42 para 2 FNA
49 art 47 FNA
50 art 3 AFMP appendix I
51 *Metock and others v Minister for Justice, Equality and Law Reform*, ECJ [25 July 2008] (C-127/08)
52 art 42 para 2 FNA; *Weisungen und Erläuterungen Ausländerbereich (Weisungen AuG)* p 240 et seq, 2013, State Secretariat for Migration (SEM)

Switzerland. This is a change from the previous minimum residence qualification of 12 years. In addition, naturalization is now only possible for foreigners who are in possession of an unlimited residence permit (C-permit). Various other aspects of the naturalization criteria have also been tightened. In a number of specific areas, the cantons are still able to make further demands as part of the naturalization process. The new law will only be applicable to applications for naturalization filed after 1 January 2018. For applications filed before this date, the existing law is still applicable.[53]

This chapter looked at the different types of residence permits and work permits available to foreigners and their families looking to settle down in Switzerland. A thorough understanding of the applicable rules and regulations is vital for a legal and successful relocation process.

Links to useful online resources

- *admin.ch/gov/en/start/federal-law/search.html*
  Provides the legislative texts referred to in this chapter
- *sem.admin.ch/sem/en/home.html*
  The State Secretariat for Migration (SEM) provides legislative texts and publishes instructions of the federal authorities that can support the understanding of legal provisions

53 Briefing Bär&Karrer, Total Revision of the Swiss Citizenship Act — Naturalization is only possible with a C-residence Permit, July 2017

About the author

THOMAS STOLTZ is a lawyer and notary. He is partner and head of notarial services and employment, migration, and social security at Bär & Karrer AG, a Swiss law firm with business establishments in Zurich, Zug, Geneva, and Lugano. Stoltz manages the Zug office. He advises national and international clients mainly located in the Zug business area on all legal issues related to corporate, commercial, and employment law. He also specializes in questions of Swiss migration law. In his capacity as civil law notary, Stoltz is regularly responsible for the notarial acts in various national and cross-border M&A transactions and IPOs assisted by Bär & Karrer. *Who's Who Legal* lists Stoltz as an expert in the area of corporate immigration.

4 Buying or Renting a Property in Switzerland

Corrado Rampini, Bär & Karrer AG

Real Estate

Persons relocating to Switzerland from abroad may buy or rent an apartment or house in Switzerland. While renting is not subject to special restrictions, the acquisition of apartments or residential houses is restricted by the Federal Law on the Acquisition of Real Estate by Persons Abroad.[1] According to this law, known simply as 'Lex Koller', foreigners may — depending on their nationality and status of residence — acquire real estate in Switzerland under certain conditions only. Moreover, construction of secondary homes is restricted by the Federal Law on Secondary Homes.

While leasing an apartment or a house in Switzerland is relatively simple, it is advisable to consult a specialist when acquiring real estate because of a number potential pitfalls.

4.1 Leasing a property

Finding a property to rent

Switzerland has a very low home ownership rate of below 40%, the lowest quota of home ownership in Europe.[2] It is therefore very common in Switzerland to lease an apartment or a house, even in the upscale or luxury markets. Despite the high number of properties in the rental market, finding a suitable, inexpensive property

1 *Bundesgesetz vom 16. Dezember 1983 über den Erwerb von Grundstücken durch Personen im Ausland* (BewG, SR 211.412.41)

2 *Bundesamt für Wohnungswesen, Wohneigentumsquoten Schweiz,* EU (2008), 2010; *bwo.admin.ch/dam/bwo/de/dokumente/01_Wohnungsmarkt/16_Zahlen_und_Fakten/163_Wohneigentumsquote/wohneigentumsquotenschweiz-eu2008.pdf.download.pdf/wohneigentumsquotenschweiz-eu2008.pdf*

may be difficult because of the low vacancy rate of below 1.5%,[3] particularly in city centers such as Zurich or Geneva. Inexpensive properties are often let even before they are publicly advertised for rental.

Today, properties for rent are offered almost exclusively on the internet.

Real estate websites
homegate.ch
immoscout24.ch
newhome.ch
urbanhome.ch
immostreet.ch
alle-immobilien.ch
comparis.ch

Many real estate agents do not accept assignments by tenants to find properties. However, specialized relocation agents assist persons relocating to Switzerland from abroad who do not speak the local language, are not familiar with local factors, seek advice, or simply do not have the time to find a property.

Relocation agents
Many relocation agents belong to the Swiss Association of Relocation Agents. Their names and contact information can be found at *sara-relocation.com*.

Negotiations and lease agreement

In general, tenancy law in Switzerland is designed to protect tenants against improper requests from landlords and abusive termination. Information on tenancy law questions from the tenants' perspective is provided by the Swiss tenant association known as *Mieterverband* (see *mieterverband.ch*).

Landlords and their property managers typically use standard agreements (for example, agreements drawn up by cantonal house owners' associations or standard agreements prepared by property managers) that often consist of a form and general terms and conditions. These standard agreements for residential properties are usually not negotiable but merely adjusted to suit the conditions relating to the leased property in question. In the upscale market, where demand is weaker and tenants

3 *Bundesamt für Statistik, Leerwohnungen* (Stand 2017); *bfs.admin.ch/bfs/de/home/statistiken/bau-wohnungswesen.assetdetail.3243383.html*

have more bargaining power, there is more room for negotiations. Prior to signing a lease, tenants should check that the lease agreement permits the property to be used for the purposes the tenant intends to use it (for example, owning pets).

For persons relocating from abroad, a few special points should be remembered:

- Lease agreements for apartments and residential properties are usually for an unlimited duration of time, and may be terminated by either side with a notice period of three months as per the dates customary in the region. In the case of a person relocating from abroad, landlords often insist on a minimum duration of one or two years to account for the higher mobility of foreigners
- Landlords often also request higher security deposits than usual (in the form of rental deposits, rental guarantees, or advance rent payments). Such requests may eventually be countered by providing a landlord with details about the background of the relocation to Switzerland
- Moreover, foreigners who are not familiar with local factors are at risk to be faced with additional requests by landlords, for example, they could be expected to take over installations or fittings installed by previous tenants, with the duty to reinstate them to their original state at the end of the lease. Tenants that leave their apartment before the end of their lease sometimes request that the new tenant buys furniture or other installations in the apartment from them. Such requests should only be accepted if the installations are really of particular value to the new tenant
- Finally, the number of cases of fraud in connection with the lease of apartments increased during the last few years, when non-existent apartments were offered for lease on real estate websites. A tenant should never make an advance payment before having ascertained that the landlord is serious and legitimate; advance payments are not common in Switzerland

4.2 Acquisition of real estate

Lex Koller

The acquisition of real estate by foreigners has been subject to an approval requirement for over 50 years. The approval requirement is regulated by the Lex Koller (also known as the 'Lex Friedrich') and the respective Federal ordinance.[4] The cantons have made introductory laws and implemented executory provision. Many communities know further legal restrictions for the acquisition of vacation homes.

4 *Verordnung vom 1. Oktober 1984 über den Erwerb von Grundstücken durch Personen im Ausland* (BewV, SR 211.412.411)

General

The Lex Koller subjects the acquisition of real estate by so-called 'persons abroad' to a permit requirement. This permit applies not only to the direct acquisition of property that is registered in the land register (i.e. the acquisition of developed and undeveloped land, condominium units, co-owned properties, etc.) but to all legal transactions that grant a person the de facto ownership of a property. The law consequently prohibits that the permit requirement is circumvented (in particular via nominees or creative contractual constructions). As a consequence, not only the agreement to, or the exercise of, a purchase right, a pre-emptive right, or a repurchase right for real estate, is subject to the permit requirement, but so are leases with very long, fixed durations, and unusual terms. The acquisition of shares in a non-listed real estate company is also subject to the permit requirement.

Who qualifies as a person abroad?

The Lex Koller applies to persons abroad. Whether a buyer qualifies as a person abroad depends on his/her citizenship (nationality),[5] and his/her status of residence.

Swiss citizens

Swiss citizens (including persons with both a Swiss and a foreign citizenship) do not qualify as persons abroad, independent of their place of residence. Swiss citizens may acquire real estate in Switzerland without any restrictions and do not require a permit.

Citizens of EU/EFTA member states

Citizens of EU/EFTA member states are treated differently depending on their countries of residence.

Citizens of EU/EFTA states with residence in Switzerland are treated in the same way as Swiss citizens. They do not qualify as persons abroad and do not require a permit for the acquisition of real estate in Switzerland. For this treatment to apply, it is required that citizens of EU/EFTA states have both their *legal* residence and their *true actual* residence in Switzerland; be it that they lived in Switzerland before, or truly relocate to Switzerland when acquiring property. Therefore, citizens of EU/EFTA states do not only require a valid residence permit (residence permit EU/EFTA B or permanent residence permit EU/EFTA C), but must also have actually moved the center of their life to Switzerland.

5 The citizenship of the spouse is irrelevant

Because of cases of misuse in the past, the Federal Office of Justice has instructed the land register authorities to investigate in detail where the buyer's center of life is, and to request evidence, for example, that the spouse or underage children live with the buyer in Switzerland, that the buyer has given notice of departure at his previous place of residence abroad, that the buyer is taxed in Switzerland, employed in Switzerland, has registered his/her vehicle in Switzerland, or participates in local clubs and associations.[6]

Citizens of EU/EFTA states with legal or actual residence abroad qualify as persons abroad and require a permit from the competent authority for the acquisition of real estate in Switzerland. Still, citizens of EU/EFTA states who work in Switzerland as cross-border commuters may acquire a secondary home in the region of their place of work.[7]

Citizens of third countries

For citizens of third counties (citizens of states other than Switzerland, the EU, or EFTA), residence status in Switzerland and permit type are deciding factors:

- Citizens of third countries who have Swiss residence and hold a permanent residence permit (C-permit) are treated in the same way as Swiss citizens. They do not qualify as persons abroad and do not require a permit to acquire real estate in Switzerland
- Citizens of third countries who have Swiss residence but do not hold a permanent residence permit (C-permit) may only acquire a house or an apartment if they will be using it themselves as their primary residence. The property must be acquired directly in the name of the buyer and may not be rented out. An indirect acquisition via a company is not permitted
  - There are no limitations in respect of the size of the property. The living area may be arbitrarily large, as long as the property comprises only one unit. Properties with a land area of over 3,000 sqm are, however, not registered directly in the land register; the buyer is referred to the competent authorities, who must assess whether the acquisition constitutes a forbidden capital investment because of the size of the property
  - If the buyer later moves house (be it that he/she leaves Switzerland or moves within Switzerland), the buyer is not obliged to sell the apartment or house and may let the property to a third party, or use it as a secondary or vacation house

6 *Bundesamt für Justiz, Erwerb von Grundstücken durch Personen im Ausland, Wegleitung für die Grundbuchämter*, Bern 2009, s 7 Ziffer 31.12

7 art 7 lit j BewG and art 18a para 3 BewV

- The buyer may also acquire a new apartment or house at his/her new place of residence in Switzerland without having to sell the first one. If, however, the foreign buyer does not intend to live in the house from the outset, this would qualify as a circumvention of the law, particularly if the buyer moves house solely for the purpose of acquiring a second home. In such a case, the competent authorities may hold that the initial acquisition would have required a permit and order that the illegal situation is remedied (through a sale of the property)[8]

In spring 2017, the Federal Council of Switzerland opened a hearing procedure for an amendment of the Lex Koller. Among other things, the Federal Council proposed to subject the acquisition of a residence by a third-state national without residence permit C to a permit requirement, making the acquisition of a primary residence by a third-state national administratively more burdensome. In addition, the Federal Council proposed that third-state nationals must sell their primary residence within two years after they leave Switzerland or stop using the property as a primary residence.

The proposals of the Federal Council are very controversial. It is therefore not foreseeable whether the proposed changes will be implemented.

- Citizens from third countries with residence abroad are considered persons abroad under the Lex Koller and require a permit by the competent authorities for the acquisition of real estate in Switzerland

Companies

Not only natural persons, but also legal entities (companies) are subject to the permit requirement under the Lex Koller. Companies with a corporate seat abroad are considered as persons abroad, even if the companies are controlled by Swiss citizens.[9] Companies that have their legal and actual corporate seat in Switzerland but are controlled by persons abroad are also considered as persons abroad.[10] Control by persons abroad is presumed by law in particular if persons abroad hold more than one third of the capital of a company, or more than one third of the voting rights, or have loaned substantial amounts to the company.[11]

A company may thus only acquire real estate in Switzerland if it has its legal and actual corporate seat in Switzerland, and is not controlled by persons abroad.

8 art 25 para 1 *bis* and art 27 BewG
9 art 5 para 1 lit b BewG
10 art 5 para 1 lit c BewG
11 art 6 BewG

Grounds to grant a permit

Buyers who qualify as persons abroad require a permit from the competent authorities to acquire real estate in Switzerland. The grounds that regulate when a permit may be granted are expressly listed in the law. If no statutory grounds to grant a permit is provided, the property may not be acquired.

Vacation homes

In terms of the number of permits, the most important grounds is for vacation homes.[12] A permit to acquire a vacation home may be granted to a person abroad if the apartment or house is situated in a community that has been designated as a tourist community by the relevant canton. Not all cantons have implemented these grounds for a permit in their legislation and designated tourist communities. In certain cantons (for example, in Zurich, Geneva, and Basel-Stadt), the acquisition of a vacation home is not possible. In addition, the number of permits granted for vacation homes is limited per canton. Each permit is counted against a quota that is assigned to the cantons by the Swiss Federation for every calendar year. Only the acquisition of properties from a foreign seller, who at the time has already bought the vacation home based on a quota, does not count against the quota.[13]

The cantons and tourist communities may impose further restrictions on permits for vacation homes. They may, for example, impose a total ban on permits for a particular place, only allowing the acquisition of condominium units, further limiting the number of permits granted per year, or only allowing the acquisition of properties that are already in foreign ownership.[14]

The cantons have designated the following communities as tourist communities:
Aargau: None
Appenzell Ausserrhoden: Bühler, Gais, Grub, Heiden, Rehetobel, Reute, Schönegrund, Teufen, Trogen, Urnäsch, Wald, Waldstatt, and Walzenhausen[15]
Appenzell Innerrohoden: None
Basel-Landschaft: None
Basel-Stadt: None

---

12 art 9 para 2 and 3 and art 10 BewG

13 art 11 BewG, art 9 BewV and annex 1 to BewV

14 art 13 BewG

15 *Appenzell Ausserrhoden: Auszug aus den Verhandlungen des Regierungsrates, Sitzung vom 11. August 2009 in Herisau ar.ch/verwaltung/departement-bau-und-volkswirtschaft/amt-fuer-wirtschaft-und-arbeit/grundstueckerwerb-durch-personen-im-ausland-lex-koller/*

Bern: In the Courtelary district: Sonceboz-Sombeval; in the Frutigen district: Adelboden, Aeschi bei Spiez, Frutigen, Kandersteg, Reichenbach; in the Interlaken district: Beatenberg, Bönigen, Brienz, Brienzwiler, Därligen, Grindelwald, Gündlischwand, Habkern, Hofstetten bei Brienz, Iseltwald, Lauterbrunnen, Lütschental, Niederried, Oberried, Ringgenberg, Saxeten, Schwanden, Unterseen, Wilderswil; in the Niedersimmental district: Diemtigen; in the Oberhasli district: Gadmen, Innertkirchen, Hasliberg, Meiringen; in the Obersimmental district: Boltigen, Lenk, Zweisimmen, St. Stephan; in the Saanen district: Gsteig, Lauenen, Saanen; in the Schwarzenburg district: Guggisberg, Rüschegg; in the Trachselwald district: Lützelflüh[16]
Freiburg: Albeuve and Montbovon, Botterens, Broc, Bulle, Cerniat, Charmey, Châtel-Saint-Denis, Châtel-sur-Montsalvens, Crésuz, Enney, Grandvillard, Gruyères, Jaun, Le Pâquier, Plaffeien, Plasselb, Pont-la-Ville, La Roche, and La Tour-de-Trême[17]
Genf: None
Glarus: All communities in the canton are considered tourist communities
Graubünden: Albula/Alvra, Andeer, Andiast, Arosa, Avers, Bergün/Bau, Bregaglia, Breil/Brigels, Brusio, Buseno, Calanca, Cama, Castaneda, Casti-Wergenstein, Cazis, Celerina/Schlarigna, Churwalden, Conters i.P., Davos, Disentis/Mustér, Domleschg, Donat, Falera, Ferrera, Fideris, Filisur, Flerden, Flims, Fürstenau, Furna, Grono, Grüsch, Ilanz/Glion, Jenaz, Klosters-Serneus, Küblis, Laax, Lantsch/Lenz, Lohn, Lostallo, Lumnezia, Luzein, Madulain, Maladers, Masein, Mathon, Medel, Mesocco, Mutten, Nufenen, Obersaxen Mundaun, Pontresina, Poschiavo, La Punt-Chamues-ch, Rongellen, Rossa, Rotenbrunnen, Roveredo, Safiental, Sagogn, Samedan, Samnaun, St. Moritz, Sta. Maria i.C., San Vittore, Scharans, Schiers, Schluein, Schmitten, Scuol, Seewis i.P., Sils i.D., Sils i.E./Segl, Silvaplana, Soazza, Splügen, Sufers, Sumvitg, Surses, Thusis, Trin, Thrun, Tschappina, Tschiertschen-Praden, Tujetsch, Urmein, Val Müstair, Vals, Valsot, Vaz/Obervaz, Waltensburg/Vuorz, Zernez, Zillis-Reischen, Zuoz[18]

16 *Bern: Anhang 1 zum Einführungsgesetz zum Bundesgesetz vom 16. Dezember 1983 über den Erwerb von Grundstücken durch Personen im Ausland* (*Stand 1. Januar 2010*) (BSG 215.126.1)

17 *Freiburg: Beschluss über die Fremdenverkehrsorte gemäss der Gesetzgebung über den Erwerb von Grundstücken durch Personen im Ausland vom 26. April 1988* (*Stand 5. Oktober 1999*) (214.12.13)

18 *Graubünden: Gemeindebestimmungen gemäss Anhang zum Regierungsbeschluss vom 16. Januar 2017* (*Stand 1. August 2017*)

Jura: Les Breuleux, La Chaux-des-Breuleux, Cornol, Courtemaîche, Les Enfers, Epauvillers and Epiquerez, Glovelier, Goumois and Les Pommerats, Montfaucon, Montfavergier, Muriaux, Le Noirmont, Le Peuchapatte, Saignelégier, Soubey, Vellerat
Luzern: Flühli and Escholzmatt-Marbach[19]
Neuenburg: In the Centre-Jura region: Le Locle, Les Brenets, Le Cerneux-Péquignot, La Brévine, La Chaux-du-Milieu, Les Ponts-de-Martel, Brot-Plamboz, La Chaux-de-Fonds, Les Planchettes, La Sagne; in the Val-de-Travers region: Val-de-Travers, La Côte-aux-Fées, Les Verrières; in the Val-de-Ruz region: Val-de-Ruz, Valangin, Rochefort and Brot-Dessous, Enges, Lignières[20]
Nidwalden: All 11 communities of the canton are considered tourist communities: Beckenried, Buochs, Dallenwil, Emmetten, Ennetbürgen, Ennetmoos, Hergiswil, Oberdorf, Stans, Stansstad, and Wolfenschiessen[21]
Obwalden: All seven communities of the canton are considered tourist communities: Alpnach, Engelberg, Giswil, Kerns, Lungern, Sachseln, and Sarnen[22]
Schaffhausen: Stein am Rhein (limited to apartments in hotel resorts)[23]
Schwyz: Arth, Illgau, Ingenbohl/Brunnen, Lauerz, Morschach, Muotathal, Oberiberg, Sattel, Schwyz, Einsiedeln district, Gersau district, and Küssnacht district[24]
Solothurn: None
St. Gallen: Alt St. Johann, Amden, Brunnadern, Bütschwil, Ebnat-Kappel, Eggersriet, Flums, Ganterschwil, Goldingen, Hemberg, Krinau, Krummenau, Lichtensteig, Lütisburg, Mels, Mogelsberg, Mosnang, Nesslau, Oberhelfenschwil, Pfäfers, Quarten, Sargans, Stein, St. Gallenkappel, St. Peterzell, Vilters-Wangs

Real Estate

19 *Luzern: Beschluss über die Bezeichnung der Fremdenverkehrsorte im Sinn des Bundesgesetzes über den Erwerb von Grundstücken durch Personen im Ausland vom 28. August 2012 (Stand 1. Januar 2013)* (SRL 219)

20 *Neuenburg: Arrêté d'exécution de la loi d'application de la loi fédérale sur l'acquisition d'immeubles par des personnes à l'étranger du 3 juillet 1985* (*Stand 1. August 2013*) (RSN 215.131.1)

21 *Nidwalden: §1 Vollzugsverordnung zum Grundstückerwerbsgesetz (Grundstückerwerbsverordnung) vom 7. September 1999 (211.31); dazu Merkblatt Erwerb von Grundeigentum (Ferienhaus/Ferienwohnung) durch Personen im Ausland der Justiz- und Sicherheitsdirektion w.ch/dl.php/de/53f6e9c64a53f/Merkblatt_Grundstuckerwerb.pdf*

22 *Obwalden: Regierungsratsbeschluss über die Förderungsorte und die Verteilung der Bewilligungen betreffend den Erwerb von Grundstücken durch Personen im Ausland für die Jahre 2017/2018 vom 8. November 2016 (Stand 1. Januar 2017)* (GDB 213.812); *dazu Merkblatt Erwerb von Grundeigentum (Ferienhaus/Ferienwohnung) durch Personen im Ausland der Justiz- und Sicherheitsdirektion ow.ch/dl.php/de/5296e80f4fd26/Merkblatt_Grundstuckerwerb.pdf*

23 *Schaffhausen: Einführungsgesetz zum Bundesgesetz über den Erwerb von Grundstücken durch Personen im Ausland vom 7. Dezember 1987* (SHR 211.412)

24 *Schwyz: Amt für Wirtschaft, Grundsätze Grundstückerwerb durch Ausländer im Kanton Schwyz* (*Stand 1. Januar 2015 bis 31. Dezember 2017*)

(Furt and Maienberg), Walenstadt, Wartau, Wattwil, Weesen (Kurzone) and Wildhaus. For apartments in hotel resorts: Bad Ragaz, Hemberg[25]

Tessin: All communities in the canton of Tessin are considered tourist communities[26]

Thurgau: None

Uri: Andermatt, Attinghausen, Bürglen, Ersteld, Flüelen, Göschenen, Gurtnellen, Hospenthal, Realp, Schattdorf, Seedorf, Seelisberg, Sisikon, Spiringen, Unterschächen, Wassen[27]

Waadt: Aigle, Avenches, Bex, Bullet, Chardonne, Château-d'Oex, Chexbres, Chavannes-près-Renens (Quartier 'Les Cèdres'), Chexbres, Corbeyrier, Gryon, L'Abbaye, La Tour-de-Peilz, Lausanne, Le Chenit, Le Lieu, Leysin, Montreux, Ollon (Les Ecovets, Chesières, Villars-sur-Ollon, Arveyes), Ormont-Dessous, Ormont-Dessus, Puidoux, Rossinière, Rougemont, Saint-Cergue, Sainte-Croix, Vevey, Veytaux, Villeneuve, Yverdon-les-Bains[28]

Wallis: the Oberwallis region with the communities Albinen, Ausserberg, Bettmeralp (Bettmeralp, Martisberg), Binn, Bister, Bitsch (Baletscha, Ebnet, Lengacher, Oberried), Blatten, Bürchen, Eggerberg, Eischoll, Eisten, Embd, Ernen (Steinhaus, Mühlebach, Ausserbinn, Ernen), Ferden, Fiesch, Fieschertal, Gampel-Bratsch (Jeizinen, Trogachra, Obere Matten, Aeggersch, Bord, Z'Opmisch Hubil), Grächen, Grengiols, Goms (Blitzingen, Niederwald, Grafschaft, Münster-Geschinen und Reckingen-Gluringen), Guttet-Feschel, Inden, Kippel, Lax, Leuk (Dorf Erschmatt, Pletschen, Oberfeithieren, Sankt-Barbara, Thel), Leukerbad, Mörel-Filet (Breiten), Naters (Birgisch, Mund, Blatten, Tschuggen, Rischinu, Täätsche, Egga, Bäll, Belalp, Geimen, Mehlbaum, Wieri, Hegdorn), Niedergesteln (Tatz), Oberems Ergisch (Zwischmatten), Obergoms, Randa, Raron (Sankt-German), Ried-Brig (Breistrasse, Bleike

25 *St. Gallen: Verordnung zum Einführungsgesetz zum Bundesgesetz über den Erwerb von Grundstücken durch Personen im Ausland vom 14. Januar 2003* (*Stand 1. Oktober 2015*) (sGS 914.11)

26 *Tessin: Legge di applicazione della legge federale sull'acquisto di fondi da parte di persone all'estero del 21 Marzo 1988* (CAN 4.1.8.1)

27 *Uri: Reglement zum Bundesgesetz über den Erwerb von Grundstücken durch Personen im Ausland vom 20. März 1985* (*Stand 1. Januar 2017*) (9.5125), *konkretisiert durch das Merkblatt zum Erwerb in den Urner Gemeinden vom 20. April 2015 secure.i-web.ch/dweb/uri/de/verwaltung/publikationen/?pubid=7807&action=info&highlight=Lex+Koller*

28 *Waadt: Règlement d'exécution de la loi d'application de la loi fédérale sur l'acquisition d'immeubles par des personnes à l'étranger du 17 Février 1987* (*Stand 1. Juni 2017*) (211.51.1), *konkretisiert durch Anhang 1 sowie Arrêté concernant l'acquisition d'immeubles par des personnes à l'étranger sur le territoire de la Commune de Chardonne du 25 Février 1998* (*Stand 1. April 2011*) (211.51.1.1) and *Arrêté concernant l'acquisition d'immeubles par des personnes à l'étranger sur le territoire de la Commune de Vevey du 1 Juni 2011* (*Stand 1. Juni 2011*) (211.51.1.2)

[Feriendorf Simplon], Wieggischmatta), Riederalp (Ried-Mörel, Greich and Goppisberg), Saas-Almagell, Saas-Fee, Saas-Grund, Sankt-Niklaus, Simplon-Dorf, Stalden, Staldenried, Steg-Hohtenn (Hohtenn), Täsch, Termen (Rosswald), Törbel, Turtmann-Unterems (Unterems), Unterbäch, Varen (Taschuniere) Visperterminen, Wiler, Zeneggen; Zwischenbergen: the Zentralwallis region with the communities Anniviers, Arbaz (Mayens d'Arbaz), Ayent (Anzère), Chalais (Vercorin), Chamoson (Mayens de Chamoson, Le Patier, Vérines, Neimia), Chermignon (Les Briesses, Crans 3 [over 1,250 m above sea level], Conthey (Le Praly), Evolène, Grône (Daillet, Erdesson, Loye, Itravers, La Coutoulaz), Hérémence (Les Collons, Les Masses, Pachié, La Comba, Ayer, Prolin, Riod, Cerise, Mâche, La Crettaz), Icogne (Assa, Crans, Plans-Mayens), Lens (Crans, Prarion, Plans-Mayens, Trionnaz), Mollens (Laques, Conzor, l'Aminona, Zironde, Clojoués), Montana (Montana-Station, Le Zotzet), Mont-Noble, Nendaz (Nendaz-Station excluding Cerisier and La Crettaz, Saclentse excluding Dorf, Magrappé, Siviez), Randogne (Vermala, Montana-Station, Bluche, Meiche, Les Barzettes), Saint-Martin, Savièse (Mayens de la Zour, Prafirmin), Sion (Les Agettes, Les Fontannets, l'Orée des Bois, Mayens de l'Hôpital, Trois Rois), Vex (Thyon 2000, Thyon Alpage, Lex Collons, Les Rindouets), Veysonnaz (except for certain zones); in the Unterwallis region: Bagnes (Verbier excluding Dorfzone, Mayens de Bruson), Bourg-Saint-Pierre, Champéry, Dorénaz (Alesse, Champex), Finhaut, Isérables, Leytron (Ovronnaz, Dugny), Liddes, Martigny-Combe (Ravoire), Monthey (Giettes, Les Cerniers, Planche, Bronnes, Vésenaux, Prafenne, Cheseaux, Sauley, Moibesset, Loëx, Le Sepey), Orsières (Maligue, Chez-les-Addy, Champex, Les Arlaches excluding Dorfzone, Branche-d'en-Bas, Praz-de-Fort ohne Dorfzone, Saleina, Branche-d'en-Haut, Prayon, La Fouly L'A-Neuve), Port-Valais (Le Bouveret), Riddes (La Tzoumaz, Villy, l'Eterpay, Villard), Saillon (Les Bains), Salvan, Saxon (over 850 m above sea level), Sembrancher (La Garde, Chamoille), St. Maurice (Mex), St-Gingolph, Trient, Troistorrents (Morgins), Vérossaz, Vollèges (Chemin, Vens, Levron, Cries, Col des Planches)[29]

Zug: None

Zürich: None

29 *Wallis: Reglement über den Erwerb von Grundstücken durch Personen im Ausland vom 21. November 2012* (*Stand 1. Januar 2016*) (211.410)

Long-term leases are not allowed for vacation homes; only short-term leases are allowed. Acquiring a vacation home solely as a capital investment is not permitted. In addition, size restrictions apply: the net residential area of a vacation home is limited to 200 m^2, and the land area to 1,000 m^2.[30] According to the practice of the Federal Office of Justice, net living areas of up to 250 m^2, and net land areas of up to 1,500 m^2, are approved, in exceptional cases even more, if a need for larger space can be proved (for example, because of the number of family members, visitors, etc.).[31]

A vacation home may only be acquired by a natural person in their own name. An indirect acquisition via a company is not permitted.[32] A person abroad may only acquire one vacation home in Switzerland. If the buyer, his/her spouse or child of less than 18 years already owns a vacation home in Switzerland, a permit may only be granted subject to the condition that this vacation home is sold prior to the registration of the acquisition of the new home in the land register.[33]

Secondary homes

In some cantons, namely in Appenzell Ausserrhoden,[34] Basel-Stadt,[35] Freiburg,[36] Graubünden,[37] Jura,[38] Luzern,[39] Neuenburg,[40] Solothurn,[41] St. Gallen,[42] Tessin,[43]

---

30 art 10 paras 2 and 3 BewV

31 Federal Office of Justice, Acquisition of real estate by persons abroad, Guidelines, Berne 2009, p 10 s, s 10 f

32 art 8 BewV

33 ar 11 para 1 BewV

34 art 1 para 1 Ziff 2 *Gesetz über die Einführung des Bundesgesetzes vom 16. Dezember 1983 über den Erwerb von Grundstücken durch Personen im Ausland vom 26. April 1987* (*Stand 1. Januar 2016*) (213.121)

35 §1 para 2 lit b *Gesetz betreffend die Einführung von weiteren Bewilligungsgründen für den Erwerb von Grundstücken durch Personen im Ausland vom 14. Januar 1988* (*Stand 1. Oktober 1997*) (214.610)

36 art 7 lit c *Ausführungsgesetz zum Bundesgesetz über den Erwerb von Grundstücken durch Personen im Ausland vom 24. September 1987* (*Stand 1. Januar 2011*) (214.12.1)

37 art 3 para 1 *Einführungsgesetz zum Bundesgesetz vom 16. Dezember 1983 über den Erwerb von Grundstücken durch Personen im Ausland vom 5. April 1987* (*Stand 1. Januar 2007*) (BR 217.600)

38 art 4 para 1 lit c *Loi portant exécution de la loi fédérale du 16 Décembre 1983 sur l'acquisition d'immeubles par des personnes à l'étranger du 22 Octobre 1987* (215.126.1)

39 §8 para 1 lit b *Gesetz zur Einführung des Bundesgesetzes über den Erwerb von Grundstücken durch Personen im Ausland vom 14. September 1987* (*Stand 1. Juli 2014*) (SRL 218)

40 art 1 lit c *Loi d'application de la loi fédérale sur l'acquisition d'immeubles par des personnes à l'étranger du 25 Février 1985* (*Stand 1. Januar 2011*) (RLN 215.131)

41 §2 para 2 *Einführungsgesetz zum Bundesgesetz über den Erwerb von Grundstücken durch Personen im Ausland vom 5. April 1987* (*Stand 1. August 2000*) (BGS 212.431)

42 art 1 para 1 *Einführungsgesetz zum Bundesgesetz über den Erwerb von Grundstücken durch Personen im Ausland vom 7. Januar 1988* (*Stand 15. Juni 2010*) (sGS 914.1)

43 art 1 lit c *Legge di applicazione della legge federale sull'acquisto di fondi da parte di persone all'estero del 21 Marzo 1988* (CAN 4.1.8.1)

Uri,[44] Waadt,[45] Wallis,[46] and Zürich,[47] a person with residence abroad may acquire a secondary home at a place to which he/she has exceptionally close ties that are worthy of protection.[48] Examples of such ties are recurring relations that a person maintains in the pursuit of commercial, cultural, or academic interests. Previous temporary stays in Switzerland (for visits, vacations, or for medical purposes), or simply having relatives in Switzerland, are not sufficient.[49]

A secondary home may not be let to a third party and must be sold within two years if the buyer stops using it as a secondary home. As in the case of a vacation home, a secondary home may only be acquired by a natural person in his/her own name, and size restrictions apply. An acquisition is only permitted if neither the buyer, nor his/her spouse, nor one of his/her children of less than 18 years already own a secondary home or vacation home in Switzerland.

Exemptions from the permit requirement

Relatives and spouses

Spouses and relatives of the seller (grandparents, parents, and children) are generally exempt from the permit requirement.[50] The acquisition of a property from such a relative does not require a permit. A permit is, however, required for a transfer in side-line (for example, between siblings). A sale of a property to the buyer's parents would thus require a permit if the parents in turn sell the property to another child shortly thereafter.[51]

Statutory heirs

Further statutory heirs under Swiss law are also generally exempt from the permit requirement if they inherit a property.[52]

44 art 1 para 1 lit b *Reglement zum Bundesgesetz über den Erwerb von Grundstücken durch Personen im Ausland vom 20. März 1985* (*Stand 1. Januar 2017*) (9.5125)

45 art 1 para 1 lit c *Règlement d'exécution de la loi d'application de la loi fédérale sur l'acquisition d'immeubles par des personnes à l'étranger du 17 Février 1987* (*Stand 1. Juni 2017*) (211.51.1)

46 art 1 para 1 lit c *Gesetz betreffend die Anwendung des Bundesgesetzes über den Erwerb von Grundstücken durch Personen im Ausland vom 31. Januar 1991* (211.41)

47 §2 *Einführungsgesetz zum Bundesgesetz über den Erwerb von Grundstücken durch Personen im Ausland vom 4. Dezember 1988* (*Stand 1. Januar 2011*) (LS 234.1)

48 art 9 para 1 lit c BewG

49 art 6 BewV

50 art 7 lit b BewG

51 Federal Office of Justice, Acquisition of real estate by persons abroad, Guridelines, Berne 2009, p 7, s 8

52 art 7 lit a BewG

Real Estate

Commercially used properties

The most notable exemption from the permit requirement applies to commercial properties. Properties that are permanently used for commercial or business purposes (office, production, logistics, retail, hotel, restaurants, etc.) are exempt from the permit requirement, and may be acquired without a permit. Such commercial properties may also be acquired as a capital investment. Beyond the sale it is irrelevant whether the property is used by the buyer himself/herself or rented to a third party for commercial or business activities.

If a residential premises is constructed, let, or traded, the property does not qualify as a commercial property.[53] The acquisition of undeveloped land in a residential, industrial or commercial zone is also subject to the permit requirement, unless construction of a building that is not subject to a permit requirement (main residence, secondary residence, or commercial building) is started within one year of the acquisition.[54]

In spring 2017, the Federal Council of Switzerland opened legal proceedings to amend the Lex Koller. The most far-reaching proposal will render commercial properties, i.e. properties used for commercial or business purposes (office, production, logistics, retail, hotel, etc.) subject to the Lex Koller again. Buyers who qualify as persons abroad would thus be excluded from acquiring commercial properties in Switzerland in the future. Only if an owner uses the property for his/her own business activities and does not let the property to a third party, an exceptional permit would be available.

This fundamental change would repeal a liberalization of the Lex Koller that was enacted in 1997. As a consequence, persons abroad would be almost completely excluded from the acquisition of real estate properties in Switzerland for investment purposes.

These proposed amendments have been heavily criticized in the hearing procedure. It is therefore not foreseeable whether and in what form the proposed changes will be implemented.

Permit procedures and sanctions

The Lex Koller is enforced by the respective cantons. Each canton has assigned one or more permit authority that decides whether a permit is required and whether the permit can be granted.

53 art 3 BewV

54 Federal Office of Justice, 'Acquisition of real estate by persons abroad', Guidelines, Berne 2009, p 6, s 6e

If a buyer cannot easily exclude that a permit is required, he/she must ask the permit authority for a permit, or ask them to hold that no permit is required.[55] The land registry authority will also refer the buyer to the permit authority if they cannot easily exclude that a permit is required; in this case the land registry sets a deadline of 30 days for the buyer to file a request for a permit, or to have it confirmed that no permit is required.[56]

Non-compliance with the Lex Koller may incur civil and criminal sanctions. Transactions that require a permit but are completed without one are considered null and void.[57] In such cases the buyer does not acquire ownership of the property, and the contract, or in particular the transfer of property and the payment of the purchase price, is not enforceable. The transaction may be reversed if already completed.[58] The avoidance of the permit requirement and false or incomplete statements vis-à-vis the competent authority or land registry authority are punishable by imprisonment of up to three years, or a fine.[59]

Acquisition process

Finding a property

Nowadays, houses and condominium properties for sale are mostly marketed on the internet on real estate websites (see section 4.1). These real estate websites provide a good overview of the properties in the market. For the sake of confidentiality, some real estate agents offer certain properties in the upscale and luxury markets only to select interested parties that they already know. Persons interested to buy a property in this market, are advised to have their names put on the mailing list of such agents.

Real estate agents in the upscale and luxury markets in German-speaking Switzerland:

- Walde & Partner Immobilien AG, Zollikon, *walde.ch*
- Ginesta Immobilien AG, Küsnacht, *ginesta.ch*
- Rudolf Steigrad AG, Zollikon, *rudolf-steigrad-ag.ch*
- Kuoni Mueller & Partner, Zurich, *kmp.ch*
- Wüst und Wüst AG, Zollikerberg, *wuestundwuest.ch*
- Engels & Völkers Wohnen Schweiz AG, Bäch, *engelvoelkers.com/ch*

---

55 art 17 para 1 BewG and art 15 para 1 BewV
56 art 18 para 1 BewG and art 15 para 3 lit a BewV
57 art 26 para 2 BewG
58 art 26 para 4 BewG
59 art 28 ss BewG

Real Estate

Negotiations and execution of the agreement

Prior to a property acquisition, it is vital to review all sales- and land-registry documentation (including all supporting documents). A visit to the property site and its immediate surroundings is essential. In the case of older properties, it is advisable to have the building's condition assessed by a specialized firm and to have a market valuation prepared.

The acquisition of real estate in Switzerland requires a public deed. The seller typically orders a draft of the agreement from the notary or land registry who sends it to the buyer for review. The notary and the land registry are independent parties in principle; they must advise both the seller and the buyer on the risks of the transaction. Because of this independence, the notary may not represent either party in the negotiations. In view of the substantial risks associated with property acquisition, it is advisable for inexperienced buyers to consult with a lawyer, even in the case of smaller properties.

A number of potential pitfalls should be considered:

- In real estate transactions in Switzerland it is normal that any legal warranty for legal or physical defects of the property is fully excluded. As a rule, the buyer thus acquires the property 'as is' and without any warranty. It is therefore important that the buyer asks the seller to give specific representations to cover the most critical points, in particular that the property is free of leases and third party rights, that no pre-emption rights or legal liens exist on the property, etc.
- Legal liens are particularly treacherous. The cantonal tax laws usually provide that the tax authorities may register a legal pledge on the property if the seller does not pay real estate gain tax or other public duties. The buyer thus usually requests that the seller has the real estate gains tax calculated by the competent tax authorities, and that the amount is directly paid to the tax authorities according to the purchase price. If this is not done, the buyer risks having to pay the seller's real estate gains tax to avoid a foreclosure if the seller fails to pay the tax
- Such legal liens also exist in other cases, in particular for claims of construction companies or workmen. Construction companies and workmen who previously worked on the property may under certain conditions have a pledge registered in the land registry if they are not paid. The buyer again risks having to pay the claims of the construction companies or workmen to avoid a foreclosure in case the seller does not pay

- In case of an acquisition of a condominium property, the condominium regulations and the decisions of the condominium owners' meeting should be reviewed; also, whether a sufficient renovation fund has been established for future renovations
- If a planned house or apartment or a house or apartment under construction is bought, it is advisable to engage a specialist to avoid additional costs. It is worthwhile to have the plans and building description checked for completeness by an architect. The acquisition of a planned house or apartment requires special provisions in the agreement to regulate the repair of defects and address any legal liens of construction companies and workmen that may follow (see above)
- Furthermore, the buyer should check that there are no contaminated sites, contaminations or waste requiring special disposal on the property, and that no harmful substances such as asbestos were used in the construction. Each canton has a register of contaminated sites where presumed contaminations and contaminated sites (but not harmful substances in buildings) are registered. In most cantons, the register is available online. Plans of other environmental risk areas such as flooding, avalanches, etc., are often available online
- Notary fees, land registry fees and cantonal and communal transfer taxes accrue in the case of an acquisition. These taxes and fees vary between cantons and communities and may be substantial. It is therefore recommended to ask a notary about accrued costs

Even prior to the signing of a public deed, sellers or their agents sometimes request the payment of a so-called 'reservation payment' to test the seriousness of the buyer's intention and to cover the costs for preparing the draft agreement. Such reservation payments often range between CHF 10,000 and CHF 50,000. Agreements for reservation payments are null and void without public notarizations, but the payments may often not be reclaimed according to judicial practice. Whoever pays such a reservation payment thus risks to lose the payment if the public deed is not signed for whatever reason.

Financing

Most Swiss banks and several insurance companies and pension funds offer financing for residential properties. Lenders prepare individual financing offers based on information on the property and affordability calculations, based on the income and wealth of the borrower, that may vary considerably from the interest rates of fixed and variable mortgage loans published in the internet. It is thus worthwhile to ask two or three institutes for offers.

Mortgage loans are secured by mortgage deeds registered to the property. Existing mortgage deeds can usually be taken over by the buyer, and should not be created anew.

4.3 Secondary homes

On 11 March 2012, the Swiss population approved a referendum initiated by an environmentalist group that wanted to restrict the construction of secondary homes. The new Federal Law on Secondary Homes and the respective ordinance came into force in 2016. According to the law, no new building permits may be issued for secondary homes in communities with a percentage of secondary homes that exceeds 20%. Over 500 communities, mostly in the tourist regions, are affected by the new regulation.

Secondary homes are apartments and houses that are used as holiday homes. The construction of such secondary homes is no longer permissible in communities that are affected by the new regulation. Only the construction of a primary home, i.e. an apartment or home that is used by a person resident in the community, remains possible. The new regulation almost brought construction in tourist regions to a halt.

The restrictions apply to all homes that were not validly approved by 11 March 2012, the date of the referendum. Older buildings are considered as 'pre-existing buildings'; such pre-existing buildings may be freely converted from a primary home to a secondary home and vice versa. A pre-existing building may even be extended if used as secondary home, but not by more than 30%.

There are only a few exceptions to the new regulation. Such exceptions exist for vacation homes that are rented to third parties on a regular and institutionalized basis, certain apartments in hotel resorts, and apartments in protected or monumental buildings. The exceptions, however, don't apply to holiday homes that are offered for rent on the internet or AirBnB only during the time that they are not used by the owner.

This chapter outlined how Swiss law regulates the renting or acquisition of real estate by foreigners in Switzerland. Those planning to relocate to Switzerland and/or purchase property there should seek the advice of a specialist to avoid potential pitfalls.

Links to useful online resources

- *gr.ch/DE/institutionen/verwaltung/dvs/giha/lexkoller/Dokumente%20lex/merkblatt_lex_e.pdf*
  Federal Office of Justice, *Acquisition of real estate by persons abroad*, Guidelines, Berne, 2009
- *gr.ch/DE/institutionen/verwaltung/dvs/giha/lexkoller/Dokumente%20lex/wegleitung_lex_d.pdf*
  Bundesamt für Justiz, Erwerb von Grundstücken durch Personen im Ausland, Wegleitung für die Grundbuchämter, Bern, 2009

About the author

DR. CORRADO RAMPINI, LL.M., is a partner and the head of the real estate practice of the Swiss law firm Bär & Karrer AG with offices in Zurich, Geneva, Lugano, and Zug. He specializes in real estate transactions of all types, including the acquisition of single properties, large-scale portfolio transactions, acquisitions of real estate companies, capital market transactions of listed real estate companies, as well as in the financing of real estate portfolios. Rampini regularly speaks at conferences about the acquisition of real estate and Lex Koller. Chambers & Partners ranks Rampini in band 1 of the leading lawyers in Switzerland for Real Estate. Legal 500 lists him among the leading individuals in the category Real Estate & Construction. He was awarded 'Lawyer of the Year 2016' for Real Estate in the Zurich area by Best Lawyers.

5 The Federal Tax System

Denise Pagani Zambelli, Altenburger

Due to its federal structure, taxes in Switzerland are levied on three levels: by the Swiss Confederation, the cantons and the communes. However, the right to collect taxes is defined and restricted by the Federal Constitution (Cst).

5.1 Basic principles of the Swiss tax system: the distribution of taxes on the three tax levels

Cantons are authorized to levy any tax that the Confederation does not claim exclusively.[1] The communes, on the other hand, may only levy income tax where they are explicitly authorized to do so by their respective cantons. In many cases the communes levy tax in the form of contributions to the cantonal tax, or they participate in the cantonal tax revenue. The three national churches (the Reformed, Roman Catholic, and Christian Catholics) raise a church tax from their members in almost all cantons.

Some items are only taxed on a single level while others are taxed at all three sovereign levels (federal, cantonal, and communal). Tax on individual income and the profit of legal entities are the most prominent examples of communal tax.

The taxes levied in Switzerland can be subdivided into direct tax (income and wealth tax for individuals, and profit and capital tax for legal entities) and indirect tax (consumption and excise tax). There are different ways to distinguish direct

1 art 3 Cst: "*The Cantons are sovereign except to the extent that their sovereignty is limited by the Federal Constitution. They exercise all rights that are not vested in the Confederation.*"

tax from indirect tax. In the case of direct tax, the calculation basis (for example, income) is generally taxed directly. For what direct tax concerns, the tax base is thus identical to the tax object.

Federal tax

Taxes on income and other direct taxes

Direct federal tax:[2]
- On the income of individuals
- On the profits of legal entities

Federal casino tax

Military service exemption tax

Consumption taxes and other indirect taxes
- Value-added tax
- Federal withholding tax
- Federal stamp duties
- Tobacco tax
- Beer tax
- Mineral oil tax
- Automobile tax
- Tax on spirits
- Custom duties

Cantonal taxes

Taxes on income and assets, and other direct taxes
- Income and wealth tax
- Poll or household tax
- Profit and capital tax
- Inheritance and gift tax
- Lottery winning tax
- Property gains tax
- Real estate tax
- Real estate transfer tax
- Trade tax

2 Federal Act on Direct Federal Taxation of 14 December 1990 (DFTA)

Property and expenditure taxes
- Automobile tax
- Dog tax
- Entertainment tax
- Cantonal stamp duty
- Lottery winning tax
- Water tax
- Miscellaneous

Communal taxes

Taxes on income and assets, and other direct taxes
- Income and wealth tax
- Poll or household tax
- Profit and capital tax
- Inheritance and gift tax
- Lottery winning tax
- Property gains tax
- Real estate tax
- Real estate transfer tax
- Trade tax

Property and expenditure taxes
- Dog tax
- Entertainment tax
- Miscellaneous

5.2 Tax harmonization

The Swiss parliament adopted the Federal Act on the Harmonization of Direct Taxation at Cantonal and Communal Levels (DTHA) on 14 December 1990 (DTHA came into force on 1 January 1993). This is a framework law that addresses cantonal and communal legislators, and stipulates the principles according to which the legislators have to set up their tax regimes in terms of tax liability, object of the tax and the tax period, procedural law, and the norms relating to tax offences.[3]

In compliance with the constitutional mandate, the DTHA specifies that the cantons remain responsible for setting tax brackets, tax rates, and tax

3 art 129 para 2 Cst; art 1 DTHA

exemption amounts.[4] The differing tax burdens originate from the fact that each of the 26 cantons has its own tax law; the levels of deductions and tax brackets vary from one canton to another, and consequently the tax burdens vary as well.

Cantonal tax examples: comparison

1. A married couple (Confessional Catholics) lives in Zurich and has no children. The pair has a taxable income of CHF 400,000 and a taxable amount of CHF 8 million.
   Total approx. amount of taxes (federal, cantonal, and communal): CHF 170,469
2. If the married couple changes residence from Zurich to Zug:
   Total approx. amount of taxes (federal, cantonal, and communal): CHF 108,785
   - The tax burden decreases by CHF 61,684
3. If the married couple changes residence from Zurich to Schwyz:
   Total approx. amount of taxes (federal, cantonal, and communal): CHF 119,661
   - The tax burden decreases by CHF 50,808
4. If the married couple changes residence from Zurich to Luzern:
   Total approx. amount of taxes (federal, cantonal, and communal): CHF 135,203
   - The tax burden decreases by CHF 35,266
5. If the married couple changes residence from Zurich to Lugano (TI):
   Total approx. amount of taxes (federal, cantonal, and communal): CHF 174,195
   - The tax burden increases by CHF 3,725
6. If the married couple changes residence from Zurich to Basel City:
   Total approx. amount of taxes (federal, cantonal, and communal): CHF 179,738
   - The tax burden increases by CHF 9,269

These different tax burdens are why inter-cantonal tax discrepancies (described as the different cantonal tax burdens that should be expected) play an important role in 'internal' Swiss relocation selection.

4 art 129 paras 1 and 2 Cst; art 1 para 3 DTHA

5.3 Overview of the most important tax types

Individual income tax

Swiss resident individuals are subject to unlimited tax liability and are taxed according to the worldwide taxation principle.

Once-off and recurring income are fundamentally subject to income tax. All cantons assess taxes in a one-year current assessment, which considers income earned. The assessment period (period in which the income underlying the tax return is earned) is the tax year. Total income is generally taxed with no distinction between the individual components or their source (exception is made for the partial taxation of dividends, see also section 5.4). Individuals pay tax on the total income they earn from self-employment, gainful employment, replacement or secondary income, as well as investment income (from movable and non-movable assets), etc.

Income includes, for example:

- Income from salaried employment and secondary activities
- Income earned on a self-employed basis (including capital gains from the sale of business assets)
- Income from pension schemes (lump-sum benefits and annuities)
- Revenue from movable and immovable property
- Other income (for example, lottery or other similar winnings of over CHF 1,000)

Gross income can be reduced by income-related expenses (so-called 'professional' expenses), general deductions (contributions to old-age and surviving dependent's insurance, disability insurance, the income compensation scheme, private debt, etc.), and social deductions (personal deductions, deduction for married persons, deductions for children, etc.). The deduction amounts vary considerably from canton to canton.

The Swiss tax system employs the principle of 'family taxation', according to which the income of married couples living together is aggregated, as from a tax perspective the family forms an economic unit. Consequently, the income of spouses living together is aggregated for tax purposes, irrespective of their matrimonial property regime.[5] The same system applies to registered partnerships since 1 January 2007.[6]

All cantons consider the family situation of taxpayers by introducing provisions for special relief measures instead of (or in addition to) deductions for married couples, or couples in a similar situation, such as single-parent families and registered partnerships.

5 art 9 para 1 DFTA
6 art 9 para 1 *bis* DFTA

The principle of joint assessment of spouses or registered partners stops applying if a couple separates. In such cases, there is also a separate assessment regardless of whether the separation was decreed by a court (factual separation is sufficient).

The tax rates applied to individual income tax are progressive. The term 'progressive' means that the rates increase as the taxpayer's income increases, up to a certain limit.

Because of the progressive income tax rates a distinction is made between average and marginal tax rates. The average tax rate corresponds to the income tax rate that is used to tax the average taxable income. The marginal tax rate, on the other hand, indicates the additional tax burden in the event of an increase of taxable income. The progressiveness of the scales varies from canton to canton.

Wealth tax

In contrast to the Swiss Confederation, all cantons and communes levy a wealth tax for individuals.

The total of a taxpayer's worldwide assets are subject to wealth tax. This includes all assets and rights that the taxpayer owns or uses. These assets and rights are generally taken into consideration at market value. Taxable assets include movable assets (for example, securities, bank deposits, automobiles, ships, planes) and immovable property. Household goods and personal belongings are, however, not taxed.

Wealth tax is calculated on net wealth. The verified amount of debts and the cantonal social allowances are deductible (some cantons guarantee a minimum amount of non-taxable wealth); the remaining net assets are subject to taxation, which is predominantly progressive and is between 0.1% and 0.9%, depending on the canton and place of residence.

Tax at source

Any Swiss-sourced income earned by a foreign citizen without a residence permit in Switzerland, is taxed at source (with a withholding tax) by all cantons.

The employer or income payer must deduct the tax due directly from the salary or payment, and has to pay this amount to the cantonal tax authority.

The deducted tax covers the income tax of the Confederation (federal direct tax), as well as the cantonal and communal taxes (including any church tax).

Expenditure-based tax

In most cantons, foreigners who take up domicile or residence in Switzerland for the first time or following an absence of at least 10 years, and who do not exercise any lucrative activity in Switzerland, can pay tax based on expenditure. The tax amount is calculated using a simplified procedure (in some cantons, payment of income and wealth tax based on expenditure) instead of paying the income tax based on the standard tax assessment.[7]

The taxpayers' and their families' annual expenditure forms the taxable basis (at least CHF 400,000 per year), and standard applicable tax rates apply.[8]

However, tax based on expenditure cannot be lower than the taxes which would be due if calculated according to the ordinary tax rates on Swiss-sourced income and assets.

In the cantons of Zurich and Appenzell Ausserrhoden, expenditure-based tax has been abolished on cantonal and communal levels.

Inheritance and gift tax

Inheritance or gifts received by individuals resident in Switzerland, and the inheritance or gifting of Swiss property, are subject to cantonal inheritance or gift tax. Inheritance and gift tax are only levied by the cantons, not by the Confederation. In some cantons, additional communal inheritance and gift tax are levied.

A transfer of assets to statutory and/or designated heirs and legatees is subject to inheritance tax, whereas gifts *inter vivos* (according to its civil law definition) are subject to gift tax.

Inheritance tax on movable assets is levied by the canton of the decedent's last place of residence; inheritance tax on immovable assets (i.e. real estate) is levied by the canton where the property is located. Inheritance tax is levied individually on the inheritance share of each heir or legatee.

Gift tax on movable assets is levied by the canton of the donor's residence; gift tax on immovable assets (i.e. real estate) is levied by the canton where the property is located.

Inheritance and gift tax are structured as once-off taxes and, as a general rule, recipients of an inheritance (heirs and legatees) or gifts (donees) are liable to pay tax in all cantons. Tax rates and eventual tax exemptions, as well as deductions or tax-exempt amounts are regulated very differently at cantonal level.

7 art 14 DFTA
8 art 36 DFTA

However, inheritance and gift tax are progressive in almost all cases and depend on the degree of kinship and/or the value of the assets in question:

- The surviving spouse or registered partner is exempt from inheritance and gift tax in almost all cantons
- Direct descendants are also exempt from inheritance and gift tax in almost all cantons

The assessment of inheritance tax follows the inventory of the *de cuiu*'s assets that must be prepared upon his/her death.

The assessment of gift tax is based on the tax return that must be prepared by the *donee* in almost all cantons.

The fact that spouses and descendants are exempt from inheritance and gift tax in most cantons is an attractive motivator for relocation to Switzerland, particularly for wealthy foreign taxpayers.

Capital gain on private movable assets

Capital gains obtained from the sale of movable private assets (for example, securities, vehicles, artwork, etc.) are tax exempt at federal, cantonal, and communal level. Exceptions are made if the sale of securities and/or real estate is made in a professional way (see section 5.6).

Property gains tax

Capital gains from the sale of privately held Swiss land or real estate are subject to cantonal property profit tax. At a federal level, these gains related to private property sales are explicitly tax exempt, but gains realized on the sale of real estate held as business assets, or realized as part of commercial immovable property trading, are taxed.

The tax burden varies depending on the canton where the real estate is located, as well as on the duration of the ownership of the property. In almost all cantons, gains realized on private real estate sales are subject to a special cantonal tax (the so-called 'property gains tax'); both individuals and legal entities are subject to this tax. Property gains tax has the characteristics of an exclusive tax in that no other property gains tax is due according to this unitary system. Capital gains on the sale of immovable properties held as business assets, or realized from commercial trading of immovable properties are, on the contrary, taxed as ordinary income or profit and are, therefore, added to other income/profits for tax purposes.

In cases where the sales price is reinvested (within a period regulated by the canton), the property gains tax can be totally or partially deferred.

Most cantons also levy a real estate transfer tax (tax on legal transactions which transfer the ownership of immovable property); the tax rates are generally proportional and vary between 1% and 3.3% of the purchase price. The buyer of the property is generally liable to tax (if no different agreement is made).

Notary and land registry fees are also regulated by the canton in which the real estate is located.

If the property or real estate is gifted or inherited, the property gains tax is deferred. Depending on the canton, in these cases the real estate transfer tax is often also not levied, or is deferred.

Federal withholding tax

Federal withholding tax is a tax withheld at source by the Confederation on revenue on movable capital assets (interests and dividends), on Swiss lottery winnings, and on certain insurance services.[9]

The tax rates are the following:

- 35% on movable capital asset revenue and on Swiss lottery winnings
- 15% on annuities and pensions
- 8% for other insurance benefits

Taxpayers with residence in Switzerland can have withholding tax refunded by filing a tax return and duly declaring the assets and related revenue subject to tax; in this sense, the withholding tax cannot be considered a 'final, definitive' tax for Swiss resident individuals. The purpose of withholding tax is to discourage domestic taxpayers from tax evasion.

For taxpayers who are resident abroad, Swiss withholding tax is a final tax burden. Only taxpayers whose country of residence has agreed a double tax treaty with Switzerland may, under determinate conditions and depending on the terms of the treaty, recover all or part of the withholding tax.

Debtors of the Federal withholding tax are the payers of income which is subject to the tax (e.g. banks, insurance companies, etc.). They must withhold the due taxes from the relevant income, and transfer it to the Federal Tax Administration (by submitting the requested statements and documents, according to the self-assessment principle).

Federal stamp duties

The Confederation levies three types of stamp duties: issuance duty, transfer duty, and duty on insurance premiums.[10]

Issuance duty is levied on the emission of domestic participation rights and corresponds to 1% of the amount accrued to a company in terms of participation

9 Federal Act on Withholding Tax of 13 October 1956
10 Federal Act on Stamp Duties of 27 June 1973

(at least of their nominal value). With regard to the issuance duty, it has to be said that there are few cases of exemption from the tax, i.e. in case of restructuring of the company (such as in case of mergers, conversions or corporation splits) and that the law also foresees an exemption limit of CHF 1 million if the issuance of non-gratuitous participation rights occurs upon the foundation or capital increase of a joint stock company or a limited liability company.

Transfer duty is levied on purchase and sale of Swiss and foreign securities (such as shares, bonds, fund shares, etc.) by domestic securities dealers. The duty amounts to 0.15% for domestic securities, and 0.3% for foreign securities. The tax is calculated based on the purchase or sale price of the securities. The Swiss securities dealer involved in the taxable transaction as an intermediary or as a contracting party, is liable to pay the tax. As with the issuance duty, the transfer duty also has few cases of exemptions from the tax.

5.4 Taxation of an important investment category: shares and participations

Gains arising from the sale of movable private assets (such as securities, paintings, vehicles, etc.) are, in principle, tax exempt (see section 5.3). In this context, however, note the subject of 'professional securities traders' (see section 5.6).

Shares

Dividend distributions by Swiss companies are subject to income tax/withholding tax of 35% (see section 5.3).

Dividend distributions by foreign companies are subject to income tax and (if foreseen) to foreign withholding tax, if the domestic tax law of the foreign country provides for such a tax.

Capital gains realized in privately held shares are free from income tax. As of 31 December of each year, the market value of shares is subject to cantonal and communal wealth tax.

Privileged dividend tax at Confederation level

Dividends, profit share, liquidation surpluses and non-cash benefits from shares, shares in limited liability companies, cooperative shares and participation certificates (including free shares, free value increases, etc.) held as business assets are taxable to the extent of 50% when such participation rights represent at least 10% of the share capital of a company or cooperative company, and have been withheld for at least one year from the taxpayer.[11]

11 art 18*b* DFTA

Privileged dividend taxation at cantonal level

The degree of mitigation is optional for the cantons within constitutional principles' limits. The tax reduction at cantonal level varies from 50% to 80% (in the majority of the cantons).

5.5 Real estate taxes

It has already been mentioned that the acquisition or sale of real estate is subject to capital gains tax, property transfer tax, and notary and land registry fees.

In approximately half of the cantons, land ownership is not only covered by the wealth tax during the period of ownership, but also by a property tax collected annually (also called land or property tax). The property tax is usually a municipal tax. If tax is levied at cantonal level, communes are generally involved with a percentage of the cantonal tax.

The tax value of the property or real estate is determined according to specific criteria. Some cantons determine the tax value according to the public land registry, while others allow the tax value to be estimated according to specific legislation. Property is taxed at the place where the property is situated without regard for the country of residence of the taxpayer. The tax is always proportional. Expressed in parts per thousand the tax rate varies from 0.2‰ to 3.0‰ of the market capitalized income or cadastral value.

If the taxpayer owns a property outside his/her canton of residence, he/she is subject to a limited tax liability in the canton where the property is situated as well, and must also submit a tax declaration in that canton.

Rental income is also subject to income tax. In the case of self-owned residential property, the cantonal tax administration establishes a theoretical rental income, the so-called 'rental value' that is also taxed as income. On the other hand, maintenance costs and debt interest rates are tax deductible.

5.6 Professional securities traders

In contrasts to the tax-exempt capital gains generated by an individual's private assets, capital gains generated by an individual who has business interests are not income tax free. The sale of investments, for example, are considered a business activity.

Tax liability is determined according to the circumstances of each individual case (see the criteria below) to establish whether a self-employed activity exists (i.e. an activity of a professional securities dealer). Tax authorities do not consider an activity as professional securities trading if the following five criteria are met:

- The holding period of the securities is at least six months
- The transaction volume (sum of all purchase prices and sales income) per calendar year amount to a total of not more than five times the securities portfolio and credit balance at the beginning of the tax period
- The capital gains from securities transactions create no need to replace missing or ceasing income to maintain standard of living. This is generally the case when the realized capital gains constitute less than 50% of net income within the tax period
- The investments are not debt financed, or the taxable income from investments (such as interest, dividends, etc.) are greater than the share of debt interest
- The purchase and sale of derivatives (especially options) is limited to the protection of own securities positions

Professional securities trading cannot be excluded if these conditions are not cumulatively met.

5.7 International tax law

If a person has ties with several countries, the question arises as to how the right to tax is differentiated between these different countries. Tax sovereignty is regulated firstly by Swiss domestic law, which determinates the terms of the right of Switzerland to tax a determinate income, or asset generated or held in the national territory.

The right to tax is delimited by international treaties (double taxation treaties, or 'DTT'). Switzerland has concluded double taxation treaties with most foreign countries.

The term double taxation is used when the taxable subject, the taxable object, and the tax period are identical and similar taxes are levied from different sovereign countries. In an international context, this happens when more than one country levies a domestic tax on a determinate income or asset of the same taxpayer for the same taxable period.

There are two methods of avoiding double taxation: the exemption method (exempting foreign income from domestic taxation) and the credit method (granting a credit on domestic tax for the foreign tax already paid).

Taxpayers who reside in Switzerland but also earn income from abroad, or who own assets located abroad are subject to special taxation rules. Switzerland taxes are levied with the 'exemption with progression' method, which means that Switzerland exempts (i.e. does not tax) determined foreign-sourced incomes and/or assets, but considers them in order to determinate the (progressive) tax rates that are applied on Swiss taxable incomes or assets.

Income tax

Unlimited and limited Swiss tax liability

Individuals who are permanently or temporary resident in Switzerland are subject to unlimited tax liability.

Tax residence is deemed to exist in the case of a stay in Switzerland (irrespective of a temporary interruption) if a person:

- Spends at least 30 days in Switzerland and is gainfully employed
- Spends at least 90 days in Switzerland and is not gainfully employed

Moreover, individuals without tax domicile or residence in Switzerland are subject to limited tax liability if there is an economic relationship between the individual and determinate tax objects (for example, real estate properties, permanent establishment of an activity, etc.) located in Switzerland.

Inheritance and gift tax

The cantons and communes are entitled to levy inheritance and gift tax. The cantonal tax laws set up tax liability on the personal (unlimited) or economic (limited) tax liability belonging to the testator or donor.

If the testator was a Swiss resident, an unlimited tax liability at his/her last domicile passes on to the heirs, encompassing the entire value of assets included in the succession inventory. If the testator was not resident in Switzerland at the time of death, the tax liability is limited to the specific asset that has a Swiss source or connection.

As a general rule, movable assets are subject to inheritance tax in the country of last domicile of the *de cuius*, and are subject to gift tax in the country of the donor's domicile at the time the gift was given. In the case of immovable assets, tax sovereignty for inheritance and gift tax lies with the country where the assets are located.

Switzerland has not entered into a double taxation treaty specifically related to gift tax with any countries, such treaties exist for the avoidance of double taxation regarding inheritance tax.

Wealth tax

Only the cantons levy a wealth tax. The tax liability is linked to the personal (unlimited) or economic (limited) tax liability affiliation.

As a general rule, immovable assets are taxed in the country where they are located. Movable private wealth is, on the contrary, basically taxable in the country of domicile of the taxpayer.

Double taxation treaties provide the same solution concerning private wealth.

5.8 Assessment and collection procedure

Assessment procedure

In Switzerland, the assessment of income and wealth tax is based on a tax return that is prepared and submitted by all taxpayers (the so-called 'self-assessment' procedure). The tax return must be completed truthfully and exhaustively and has to be returned to the competent authority within the deadline determined by the relevant canton. In general, an extension can be requested. If taxpayers do not submit their tax returns, an *ex officio* assessment is undertaken by the tax authorities.

Once the assessment authority has received the duly completed and signed tax return, together with the required enclosures, the various tax factors can be determined (taxable income and wealth, tax rates, and the tax amount).

The taxpayer receives a notification of the assessment by means of a written ruling. This ruling contains the decisive tax factors, as well as the tax amount for the tax year in question. It also indicates the possible legal remedies, the form, the time frame to be observed, and the authority to which an eventual objection can be addressed.

If no valid objection to the notified assessment decision is proposed, the assessment decision enters into force. Legally binding assessments can, however, be changed to the detriment of the taxpayer by a supplementary tax procedure if it subsequently transpires that they are insufficient or incorrect, for example, due to tax evasion or tax fraud. They may also be changed in a taxpayer's favor if new reasons or evidence justify a revision.

As a rule, the communes use the same assessment basis and the same tariff as the cantons, whereby the communes levy these taxes as a multiple of the cantonal basic tariff, or as a multiple of the effectively owed state tax.

Collection procedure

The collection of income and wealth tax from individuals is generally carried out by the same office that issued the tax assessment.

While direct federal tax is generally collected by the cantonal tax administration, the collection of cantonal and communal taxes differs. Tax collection can be partly carried out by a specific cantonal office, partly by the commune of residence of the taxpayer, or cantonal taxes can be collected by the canton and communal taxes by the communes.

Taxes must be paid by determinate due dates. In the case of direct federal tax, the due date is generally 1 March of the year following the current tax year.

In most cantons, cantonal and communal taxes are collected in several provisional installments during the tax year. The balance (i.e. the difference between what has already been paid and the total amount that is due from the taxpayer), either still must be paid or is refunded to the taxpayer as soon as the tax assessment comes into force.

First-time assessment after relocation to Switzerland

If relocating from abroad the tax liability in Switzerland begins on the date of arrival i.e., on the day of personal registration at the communal office. If relocation takes effect by 1 January the taxpayer will be properly assessed in the first year of relocation.

Residence under one year

If relocation from abroad occurs during the year taxes are levied only for the period that the relocated person lived in Switzerland (since the tax period is not complete).

Income tax is levied only on the income effectively earned during this period. To determine the tax rate regular income is converted to 12 months (so-called 'annualization'). Property is taxed according to its situation from 31 December of the year of the relocation to Switzerland.

This chapter set out to explain the three different levels at which taxes are levied in Switzerland: federal, cantonal, and communal. As discussed, taxes can further be subdivided into direct tax and indirect tax. The tax liability may be unlimited or limited according to the residence and personal situation of the taxpayer, and the tax rates are, for the majority, determined progressively at all three levels. It is therefore important to understand the complicated taxation system before relocating to Switzerland.

Links to useful online resources

- *estv.admin.ch*
  Official website of the Federal Tax Administration, Bern (Switzerland)
- *swiss-tax.ch*
  The Internet platform *Swiss tax law on the Internet* is a comprehensive collection of links to the tax laws of the Confederation and the cantons as well as other relevant information
- *steuerkonferenz.ch* and *steuer-easy.ch*
  Official website of the Swiss Tax Conference. The Swiss Tax Conference deals with questions of tax law and litigation, and calls for efforts to ensure the smooth running of business transactions between tax administrations

References

IBFD, *Global Individual Tax Handbook* (2016 edn, Amsterdam, The Netherlands)
Oberson X., *Droit fiscal Suisse* (IV edn, 2012, Basel, Switzerland)
Swiss Tax Conference, *The Swiss tax system* (2017 edn, Bern, Switzerland)

About the author

DENISE PAGANI ZAMBELLI is a Swiss attorney-at-law with a Master of Advanced Studies (M.A.S.) in Tax Law. She is admitted at the Ticino Bar Association (OATi), the Swiss Bar Association (FSA), the International Bar Association (IBA), and is also a member of the Swiss Branch of the International Fiscal Association (IFA). Her practice focuses prevalently on tax law, but she is also active in other areas such as commercial and corporate law, as well as immigration and labor law. She also advises on cross-border questions between Italy and Switzerland.

6 Taxation of Legal Entities

Michael Barrot, Bratschi

Switzerland's mild tax climate for companies, entrepreneurs, and individuals, together with the advantage of binding advance tax rulings in general, makes the country a preferred destination for any kind of international business.

6.1 Legal forms of business organization

Most businesses in Switzerland are organized in the form of Swiss corporate entities. Furthermore, many foreign companies also make use of Swiss branches to conduct their business in Switzerland. If these branches are considered as permanent establishments (PEs), they are treated in the same way as Swiss companies for tax purposes, but they are not subject to Swiss withholding tax.

Corporate

The most popular and widespread type of business entity under Swiss law is the corporation, also called company limited by shares (*Aktiengesellschaft* — AG), whereas a smaller business is usually organized in the form of a limited liability company (*Gesellschaft mit beschränkter Haftung* — GmbH). Limited liability companies (LLCs) are often used by US groups, as LLCs qualify for 'check the box' rules from a US tax perspective.

LLC enterprises have their own name, their own legal personality separate from their members, and a fixed nominal capital divided into shares. The shareholders' personal liabilities are generally limited to the full payment of the nominal value of their shares. The formation of an LLC requires the adoption of related resolutions by the founder(s), the minutes of which are to be established in the form of a public deed (to be notarized), followed by the registration of the new legal entity in the commercial register of the respective canton.

The relevant differences between a corporation and an LLC are as follows:

- The minimum amount of share capital for a corporation is CHF 100,000; for an LLC it is CHF 20,000
- A corporation can have registered or bearer shares, whereas an LLC is limited to registered shares only
- The articles of association of an LLC can be more restrictive with respect to transfers of shares than those of a corporation

A corporation's corporate body consists of the shareholders, the board of directors, and the auditors. Swiss corporate law does not provide for a further body or level of 'officers'. If certain thresholds are not met, the legal entities are subject to a limited audit, or can opt out of the audit requirement.

Non-corporate

Swiss company law provides for general and limited partnerships. However, only smaller businesses run by individuals and a few private banks use these forms of partnerships. This is because Swiss corporate law requires that all general partners of a general or limited partnership must in almost all cases be individuals. Swiss partnerships are usually treated transparently for Swiss tax purposes.

6.2 Tax residence and fiscal domicile

Corporate residence

Legal entities, i.e. corporations, LLCs, cooperatives, associations and foundations, are subject to Swiss federal, cantonal, and communal corporate income tax if they are resident (i.e. if they are incorporated or effectively managed and controlled) in Switzerland.

Branch or permanent establishment

Legal entities not incorporated in but effectively managed and controlled in Switzerland are subject to Swiss federal, cantonal, and communal corporate income tax if they have a permanent establishment (PE) or a fixed place of business located in Switzerland. Therefore, any profits and gains attributed to such a PE or fixed place of business of a foreign corporate entity, are treated the same way as described for Swiss tax-resident legal entities. However, as there are no dividend distributions from a PE or a fixed place of business, the Swiss withholding tax does not apply with regard to the repatriation of funds.

In order to avoid qualifying as a PE or a fixed place of business, such local business presences should have no authority to conclude or negotiate contracts in the name of the foreign legal entity and their activities should be strictly limited to marketing and promotion.

6.3 Overview of the Swiss tax system applicable to corporate taxpayers

The Swiss tax system

Switzerland has a highly federalist structure, which is also evident in its taxation system. According to the Swiss Constitution, the 26 cantons have fiscal sovereignty and the full right of taxation, to the extent that the right to tax a particular source is not exclusively allocated to the Swiss federal government in the Federal Constitution. As a consequence, Switzerland has two levels of corporate taxation — the federal and the cantonal respectively communal levels.

While the levying of certain, primarily indirect taxes (for example, value-added tax (VAT), stamp duties, withholding tax on dividends, etc.) is reserved to the Swiss federal government, other — primarily direct taxes on income — are levied not only by the Swiss federal government, but also at the levels of the cantons and the communes. The legislative power of cantonal and communal taxes generally lies with the legislative bodies of the 26 cantons. Although a federal law aiming at harmonizing the cantonal tax laws in certain respects exists, there is still a considerable variety of different cantonal tax systems and rules. To date, endeavors to harmonize cantonal and communal tax rules have not included rates of taxation. As a result, the effective income and capital tax burden varies considerably from canton to canton and even between the communes of one given canton.

The codified tax law at the different levels (federal, cantonal, and communal) is not very detailed compared to the tax legislation of many other industrialized countries. Hence, tax administrations at the different levels enjoy a considerable degree of discretion in the application of tax laws. These laws are open enough to allow the cantonal authorities (within certain limits) to enter into private rulings with corporate taxpayers subject to their tax jurisdiction.

Corporate Income Tax

Determination of taxable income

Swiss companies are liable for federal, cantonal, and communal taxes on their worldwide income. In general, there is no distinction between the taxation of income and capital gains at company level. However, certain differences may occur in connection with the participation exemption regime (see section 6.4).

Income and capital attributed to a foreign PE or foreign real estate is exempt from Swiss taxation; however, it is taken into consideration for determining the applicable cantonal or communal tax rate in those cantons that apply a progressive corporate income tax rate.

The income tax liability of each resident company of a group of companies (whether Swiss or foreign controlled) is calculated on the basis of the net profit shown in its statutory financial statements (*Massgeblichkeitsprinzip*, subject to possible adjustments for tax purposes). If the company does not comply with the Swiss tax accounting principles in preparing its statutory financial statements, certain differences in the timing of recognition of specific profits and losses for tax purposes may occur.

As a rule, the standard federal taxes of a company account for approximately one third, and the combined cantonal and communal taxes for approximately two thirds, of the total direct tax burden, depending on the corporation's canton and commune of residence.

Loss carryforward rules

Swiss companies may offset generated profits against losses incurred during the preceding seven years (tax loss carryforward). In the event of recapitalization, respective gains from the waiver of debt might be offset for extended periods.

Losses may survive a change of ownership, if the change in ownership was not motivated solely by existing losses but rather by commercial interests.

Rates

At federal level, corporate taxpayers are subject to a flat rate of 8.5% on their taxable income (net profit). According to Swiss tax law, tax charges can be deducted from taxable income. As a result, an effective tax rate of 7.83% is applied to annual net profit.

The cantons and communes can establish their tax rates at their own discretion according to Swiss tax legislation. The aggregate effective corporate federal, cantonal and communal corporate income tax rate may vary between approximately 12.4%–24.2%.

Administration

A corporate tax return has to be filed on an annual basis within three months of completion of the relevant business year. Extensions for filing later are available and widely used. During the business year, provisional taxes may be due, which are usually invoiced on an estimate basis (down payments) or have to be provisioned for in the company's accounts.

Swiss tax law does not foresee a specific pre-scheduled cycle for tax audits. However, each company is subject to an audit from time to time.

Tax grouping

Swiss tax law does not foresee a tax grouping or a loss consolidation for corporation tax purposes. Each company has to draw its own financial statements and file its own tax returns on a stand-alone basis. Only losses incurred at the level of PEs (including abroad) may be deducted from the taxable profit. Losses from a foreign PE may be recaptured in order to avoid a double deduction of losses abroad, and in Switzerland itself. Conversely, a Swiss PE cannot offset foreign headquarter losses against profits attributable to this PE.

Capital tax

Corporate capital tax is a cantonal and communal tax levied on the net capital, consisting of paid-in share capital, surplus and retained earnings, or on the dotation capital of Swiss PEs of foreign companies. No such tax exists at federal level. The capital tax rate varies from canton to canton and is dependent on the tax status of the company. It ranges between 0.067%–0.9% for companies subject to standard taxation, and between 0.005%–0.176% for tax-privileged companies.

Stamp duties

The contribution of equity to a Swiss company is generally subject to a capital-issuance stamp duty at a rate of 1% of the fair market value of the assets paid or contributed. Exemptions from the 1% stamp duty may, however, are available in cases of corporate reorganization (mergers, spin-offs, etc.), certain financial restructurings, and where a corporate entity that was originally incorporated abroad moves its registered seat and domicile to Switzerland. Furthermore, the first CHF 1,000,000 of contributed capital is exempt from stamp duty.

The transfer of securities issued by a Swiss or foreign issuer for a consideration is subject to the securities-transfer stamp duty if at least one of the parties to, or an intermediary in the transaction is a qualified Swiss securities dealer. The transfer stamp duty is calculated on the consideration paid; the tax rates are 0.15% for Swiss, and 0.3% for foreign securities.

Value-added tax

Switzerland imposes VAT as an indirect tax on most goods and services and it applies to each stage of the production and distribution chain. VAT is designed as a supplier liability based tax (i.e. the liability is calculated on the consideration paid by the recipient).

The standard VAT rate is 8%. Goods and services are generally subject to this rate. A 3.8% rate is levied on services in connection with the provision of accommodation, including breakfast. A 2.5% rate is levied on certain basic necessities such as delivery of water, food, non-alcoholic drinks, medicine, newspapers, fees for non-commercial TV and radio broadcasting, etc.

Swiss VAT regulations provide that any person or legal entity (for example, a subsidiary, branch, or sole trader) performing an income-producing commercial, professional or non-profit oriented activity is required to register for and to charge VAT, if the total of supplies of goods, services and consumption on Swiss territory and abroad exceeds CHF 100,000 per annum.

Withholding tax

The Swiss federal government levies a withholding tax of 35% on the gross amount of:

- Dividends, including constructive and liquidation dividends distributed by a Swiss company

- Interest paid on publicly offered bonds, debentures, and other instruments of indebtedness issued by a borrower resident in Switzerland
- Distributions by a Swiss investment fund
- Interest on customers' deposits with a Swiss bank

There is, however, no withholding tax on interest paid in connection with straight-term loans, rent, royalties and fees regarding licences, management and technical assistance, and no withholding tax is levied on dividends paid from additional paid-in capital.

Switzerland has concluded bilateral tax treaties with more than 90 countries including the US, Canada, Japan, and most of the countries in Europe. Furthermore, a full withholding tax relief applies to dividends paid by a Swiss company to a parent company resident in any EU member state, if the parent company holds at least 25% of the shares of the Swiss company for at least two years, and vice versa, as well as a full withholding tax relief on interest and royalties.[1]

Switzerland follows the exemption method pursuant to the Organisation for Economic Co-operation and Development (OECD) Model Convention[2] and grants a tax credit for foreign residual withholding taxes, provided a respective double taxation treaty is applicable.

6.4 Tax incentives, special regimes, and relief that may encourage inward investment

Participation exemption relief

A tax relief applies to dividend income of companies resident in Switzerland derived from substantial participations. A participation is considered substantial if it represents a control of at least 10% of the share capital, or 10% of the profit entitlements of another company, or if it has a fair market value of at least CHF 1,000,000. The participation exemption is not an outright tax exemption, but rather a tax abatement mechanism. Qualifying dividend income may benefit from the 'participation deduction' (*Beteiligungsabzug*), which is equal to the ratio between the net participation income and the total net income of the corporation.

The net participation income consists of the gross dividend income from substantial participations, less non-refundable foreign withholding taxes and financing costs related to the respective participations, and 5% of the dividend income for covering

1 art 9 Switzerland-EU Savings Tax Agreement
2 art 23A OECD Model Convention

administrative costs. In most cases, the participation exemption results in a full (or close to full) exemption of participation income from federal income tax.

The deduction ratio so determined is applied to the amount of income tax calculated on the total net profit, including the qualifying dividend income. The participation deduction is not granted to the extent that the book value of the underlying participation is amortized as a consequence of the dividend distribution.

The participation exemption relief can also be claimed in respect of realized capital gains if the participation sold represents at least 10% of the other companies' capital and has been held for at least one year. The capital gain qualifies for the *Beteiligungsabzug* only to the extent that the sales proceeds exceed the cost value of the participation. Any portion of the gain representing recaptured depreciation, does not qualify.

Holding company regimes

Holding companies are exempt from cantonal and communal corporate income tax in all Swiss cantons, provided the following requirements are met:

- The purpose of the company as stated in the articles of association is the holding and management of participations in affiliated companies
- The income deriving from the participations equals at least two thirds of the total income generated by the company, or those two thirds of the assets as stated in the balance sheet consist of qualifying participations
- The company is not engaged in any commercial activities in Switzerland

The cantons may accept certain minor activities, in particular management, administration and licensing, but this varies from canton to canton.

Like all other legal entities subject to federal corporate income tax, holding companies are taxed with 7.83% on annual net profit. However, the participation relief as described above can also be claimed at federal level, leading to an almost total exemption of dividends and capital gains from taxation.

Domicile company regime

Domicile (administration, mixed or auxillary) company regimes are legal entities that do not conduct any (or only conducts a limited amount of) business activities within Switzerland. A domicile company has no employees and no office infrastructure in Switzerland, and carries out all of its business abroad. A mixed, administration or auxiliary company may have offices and personnel in Switzerland, and may carry out support functions or minor trading activities in Switzerland, but these functions or activities must be subordinate to the company's non-Swiss business. A mixed company must derive at least 80% of its gross income from non-Swiss sources (for example, trading with foreign counter parties) and should generally incur at least 80% of its expenses (including costs of goods sold) outside of Switzerland.

Swiss companies (and branches or foreign companies) with these characteristics are eligible for special tax treatment at the cantonal and communal level (no particular tax status exists at the federal level). Standard income from Swiss sources is subject to standard cantonal and communal taxation. Standard income from non-Swiss sources is partly exempt from tax (typically between 70%–90%). Income and gains from substantial equity investments in other corporate entities are fully exempt from tax. The effective tax rate of such companies is usually in the range of 8%–11%.

State aid

Industrial or commercial enterprises moving to Switzerland from abroad may, in almost all cantons, be granted a partial or even a full exemption from cantonal or communal tax, and in certain defined geographical areas with low economic growth, also from federal income and capital tax for a maximum duration of 10 years. Such exemptions must be negotiated with the cantonal authorities and generally require that a substantial number of new jobs is created in a region with a high unemployment rate.

6.5 Taxation of funding structures

Thin capitalization

The Federal Tax Administration issued a circular letter on 6 June 1997 on the criteria for hidden equity capital. This letter lays down detailed thin capitalization rules for purposes of direct federal tax. The total debt provided by shareholders or affiliated parties should not exceed the aggregate (market) value of the following assets of the company, as the case may be, reduced by the total interest-bearing debt capital from independent third parties (such as banks) at the end of the year:

- 100 % of cash
- 90 % of Swiss and foreign bonds issued in Swiss francs
- 85 % of loans and advances, receivables on supplies and services
- 85 % of inventory
- 85 % of other current assets
- 80 % of foreign bonds issued in foreign currencies
- 70 % of participations
- 60 % of Swiss and foreign shares listed on a stock exchange
- 50 % of other shares/investments in limited liability companies
- 70 % of operating real estate
- 70 % of private real estate, holiday homes and zoned land
- 80 % of other immovable property
- 50 % of machinery and equipment
- 70 % of other intangible assets

As a general rule, finance companies may have a maximum debt-to-equity ratio of 6:1, whereas holding companies are subject to the debt-to-equity financing rules mentioned above. These rules can be overruled by an arm's length assessment. The excess debt finance is deemed to be equity if it is provided by a shareholder, or someone close to him/her, or if it is guaranteed by such a person while being provided by a third party. Interest on deemed equity is not deductible for corporate income tax purposes and, in addition, is subject to 35% withholding tax (qualifies as constructive dividend).

For the calculation of excess interest, the maximum debt amount is multiplied by the maximum safe harbor interest rate published by the Federal Tax Administration on a regular (usually annual) basis. Only if the effective amount of interest paid is higher than the maximum amount calculated in accordance with the formula mentioned above, will an adjustment to taxable profits and a re-characterization into a dividend be made.

Deduction of finance costs

Finance costs (for example, interest payments) paid to third parties are usually deductible for tax purposes. Payments of finance costs to related parties, however, have to comply with the thin capitalization rules (see above) and the maximum interest rates annually published by the Federal Tax Administration. For 2018, a maximum interest rate of 0.75% (holding companies) and 1% (trade and industrial companies) is accepted for loans granted over CHF 1 million. Different interest rates apply for foreign currencies.

Restrictions on payments

Swiss tax authorities consider interest payments on debt exceeding the thin capitalization rules, as well as interest payments in excess of the minimum interest rates, as hidden profit distribution subject to withholding tax at a rate of 35%.

Return of capital (capital contribution principle)

According to the capital contribution principle, all contributions (i.e. share capital, but also additional paid-in capital) to a legal entity may be repaid to the shareholder free of withholding tax. In addition, such a return of capital is exempt from income tax for individuals resident in Switzerland holding their shares as private assets. However, qualifying additional paid-in capital has to be separately accounted for in the accounts in order to benefit from this regulation.

6.6 Acquisition structures, restructuring, and exit charges

Acquisition

Swiss tax regulations do not foresee a group taxation regime. As such, any interest payments paid in connection with acquisition finance costs pushed down to the target company, will not be accepted by most cantons as deductible expenses for the first five years following the acquisition. As an alternative, the acquiring company may indirectly push down part of the acquisition finance costs through a capital reduction or a distribution of reserves of the target company, which is in principle accepted.

Reorganization

Swiss taxation law contains specific provisions that provide for tax-neutral group reorganizations for all applicable Swiss taxes such as corporate income tax, withholding tax, stamp duties, income tax at shareholder level, real estate capital gains taxes, real estate transfer taxes, and VAT.

Exit (corporate migration)

Under Swiss tax law, the exit of a Swiss company from Switzerland is regarded as a liquidation for withholding tax purposes. As such, withholding tax is due on the so-called liquidation proceeds, which is the difference of the market value of the assets, and the nominal value, including any of the company's additional paid-in capital reserves. In addition, the difference between the market and the book value of the assets is subject to corporate income tax, provided that the assets will leave Swiss territory.

6.7 Anti-avoidance and other relevant legislation

General anti-avoidance

In 1962, Switzerland introduced an anti-abuse decree on a unilateral basis, which applies to outbound investments of companies resident in Switzerland. This decree ensures that mere conduit companies do not have access to the extensive Swiss double taxation treaty network. The decree provides in particular for minimum distribution requirements regarding certain companies.

A general anti-avoidance doctrine based on case law of the Swiss Supreme Court, is applied by the Federal Tax Administration on inbound investments. In the event of treaty shopping, the Federal Tax Administration refuses to refund the withholding tax deducted from dividend distributions.

Transfer pricing

Switzerland follows the OECD model transfer pricing guidelines. Apart from these guidelines, Swiss tax law does not provide for any additional transfer pricing regulations or documentary requirements, which have to be taken into consideration with regard to intra-group transactions.

Tax clearance and rulings

Switzerland is very well known for its advance tax ruling practice. This practice is often used to obtain certainty with regard to the tax treatment of a specific transaction. Usually, the tax ruling procedure takes just a few weeks and is a regular part of the overall transaction. The Swiss tax authorities at federal as well as cantonal and communal levels are bound by a valid tax ruling, as long as the facts and circumstances have been properly documented.

6.8 Corporate Tax Reform Act III and tax proposal 17

The third series of corporate tax reforms (CTR III) was intended to abolish the reduced taxation of holding, domiciliary and mixed companies, as this reduced taxation is no longer in line with international standards. To prevent a loss of competitiveness for Switzerland, internationally accepted tax relief measures were introduced, with a focus on the promotion of innovation. A referendum was held on the proposed reform. Opponents of the reform expected significant losses of tax receipts, and it was rejected by the people and the cantons on 12 February 2017.

About half a year after the failure of the CTR Ili, the Federal Council proposed a new version of the project with its tax proposal 17. The consultation process on the Federal Council's revised tax proposal 17 was concluded in December 2017. The Federal Council drew up the bill based on responses received during the consultation process on the revised tax proposal. This bill is supported by the cantons as well as the cities and communes and was forwarded to parliament for discussion in March 2018. The bill includes the following measures:

- Abolishment of the current preferential cantonal tax regimes (holding, domiciliary, and mixed company status). The Federal regimes (Swiss finance branch and principal company) shall be abolished via changes in practice
- Introduction of a mandatory cantonal patent box regime which complies with the OECD's modified nexus approach. The patent box will be available in cases of patents or comparable rights. The maximum tax relief available for respective IP income will be limited to 90%. Cantons may opt for a less extensive relief
- The option for cantons to introduce a super-deduction of up to 50% on certain Swiss R&D expenses. Such Swiss R&D expenses would be personnel expenses directly allocated to R&D plus 35% of other R&D personnel expenses. Furthermore, 80% of the fees paid for (Swiss) contract research will also qualify for the super-deduction
- The aggregated reductions of the tax basis through the patent box, additional deduction for R&D expenditures and a step-up tax depreciation stemming from an early exit from a current tax regime in accordance with current cantonal practice shall not exceed 70%. Cantons may introduce lower thresholds of the relief limitation

- Permanent establishments of foreign companies that are subject to ordinary income and capital taxation in Switzerland may benefit from a tax credit on foreign source taxes, which is currently available for legal entities only. The cantons may implement a reduction of the portion of taxable equity relating to investments and qualifying patents
- The 5% threshold applicable to shares transferred to a self-owned company will be abolished. Accordingly, the transfer or sale of any shares, regardless of the amount or stake held, could result in taxable income at the level of the individual shareholder
- As a counter-financing measure, the Federal Council proposes to increase the minimum taxation of qualifying dividend income earned by individuals who are resident in Switzerland to 70% at the federal level, and at least 70% at the cantonal level
- The transitional rules foresee that hidden reserves (including goodwill) will be subject to a separate, reduced taxation over a 5-year period, to the extent that they have not been subject to income taxes in Switzerland to date. The relevant applicable tax rate is at the discretion of the cantons
- Companies or business functions that migrated to Switzerland from abroad may benefit from a step-up of hidden reserves (including goodwill) up to the fair market values in the tax balance sheet in the first tax return
- To compensate the cantons for the losses in tax revenue expected to arise from the proposed changes in legislation, the Federal Council further proposes to increase the share of the cantons in federal income tax revenue from the current 17% to 21.2%
- Finally, the proposal also provides for an increase of the minimum family allowance by CHF 30 per month. This means that child allowances will rise to at least CHF 230 and education allowances will rise to at least CHF 280. In this regard, about 18 cantons will need to increase their payments

Parliament will make its decision on the proposal in the autumn of 2018. If no referendum is called, the first tax proposal 17 measures will come into force on 1 January 2019, whereas most of the measures will come into force on 1 January 2020.

6.9 International tax policies

Switzerland supports international efforts to achieve greater transparency and a level playing field with regard to the taxation of multinationals. As a member of the OECD, Switzerland actively participated in the base erosion and profit shifting (BEPS) project. The Federal Council has instructed the Federal Department of Finance (FDF) to deliver analyses and proposals for implementing the outcomes of the BEPS project.

Some outcomes are regarded as new minimum standards to which all G20 and OECD member states undertake to comply. The minimum requirements concern country-by-country reports, criteria for taxing intangible property (patent boxes), the spontaneous exchange of information on advance tax rulings, access to the mutual agreement procedure for resolving disputes, and the inclusion of anti-abuse clauses in double taxation agreements. With the so-called 'inclusive framework', the OECD has established a control system to monitor member states' compliance with the minimum requirements.

With tax proposal 17, Switzerland should align its corporate tax law with international standards and abolish tax regimes that are no longer accepted internationally. In this way, the declaration of intent of the Federal Council and of the 28 EU member states of October 2014 will also be implemented. Switzerland is currently in the process of implementing other international standards stemming from the BEPS project; Switzerland will have the necessary legal basis with regard to the spontaneous exchange of information on tax rulings from 1 January 2018, with the OECD/Council of Europe multilateral administrative assistance convention. The statutory basis for the exchange of country-by-country reports is also being prepared. These country-by-country reports will allow for a general overview of the worldwide distribution of multinational profits and taxes.

This chapter has provided an overview of Switzerland's tax legislation for companies, entrepreneurs, and individuals. It also considered the international tax context and explained what measures Switzerland intends to implement in the near future to be more transparent and aligned with international standards.

About the author

MICHAEL A. BARROT graduated from the University of Bern in 2002, was admitted to the Zurich Bar in 2005, and joined a renowned law firm in Zurich as an associate in the same year. In 2007 he received his Master of Law (LL.M.) from the University of California, Los Angeles, and he became a Certified Tax Expert in 2010. In April 2014 he joined Bratschi as a tax partner. He is a member of the Swiss Bar Association, the Zurich Bar Association, the Swiss Institute of Certified Accountants and Tax Consultants, the International Fiscal Association, and the Swiss Association of Certified Tax Experts. Michael A. Barrot specializes in domestic and international tax. He advises Swiss and international companies on corporate reorganizations, real estate and capital market transactions, as well as employee participation programs. Other areas of expertise include tax planning for Swiss and foreign private clients and domestic tax litigation. He is part of the taxation and transaction practice groups, as well as the financial services industry group.

7 Lump-sum Taxation in Switzerland

Robert Desax, Walder Wyss

Recent years have seen general tendencies in the areas of taxation, the banking industry, and the general state of public finances in Europe that are increasingly becoming a cause of concern to many. We have witnessed the introduction of new rules on financial transparency and exchange of information, and a proliferation of new regulations and compliance requirements. Tax increases loom on the horizon in numerous countries. Various 'leaks' exposing confidential information of private individuals are released to the public domain by the media on a regular basis. In addition, a perceived mobilization of public opinion against 'the rich' as well as mounting concerns over the incessant inflation of public debt levels have contributed to growing general uncertainty for many wealthy individuals and families.

In the UK, for example, these developments have led the government to introduce new measures that will directly impact non-domiciled residents negatively. Most notably, the 'non-dom' status will no longer be indefinite. The Brexit vote of June 2016 has amplified existing concerns about the mid-term future.

With all these developments in mind, many wealthy families across the globe are seeking to put contingency plans in place. Many are already willing to 'vote with their feet', and to establish themselves in a new country. They are generally looking for stability, predictability, privacy and, of course, moderate levels of taxation.

Switzerland has had its share of many of the aforementioned developments (especially in the banking and corporate tax areas). The willingness and ability of the relevant political actors to maintain the country's traditional allure for wealthy individuals and to remain a reliable partner, has never been stronger. Be it the upholding in 2014 of traditional lump-sum taxation for private individuals in most Swiss cantons (almost 60% in favor), or the rejection in 2015 by a large majority (71%) of the voters of a general 20% estate and gift tax that would have penalized direct descendants (who generally benefit from full tax exemption), Swiss voters have systematically and consistently refused to approve invasive proposals aimed at increasing the tax burden on the wealthy. As a more recent example, in a public referendum in June 2016 a clear majority of the population in Geneva decided to maintain lump-sum taxation for foreigners.

Switzerland is composed of 26 cantons (states), each of which is financially autonomous. The cantons are in charge of their own budgets, and they set their own tax rates. As a consequence, robust tax competition exists among the cantons and there are notable differences in their respective tax rates.

The taxpayer-friendly environment is, however, not only ensured by an attractive framework of tax rules, but also by the fact that, unlike its neighbors, the ratio of public debt to GDP in Switzerland has been continuously reduced over the last few years and is now at a low of 33.1% (the Maastricht debt limit being set at 60%). Arguably, public debt is fundamentally just postponed taxation. Thus, the moderate level of Swiss public debt should ensure that the country will be able to maintain its appeal to taxpayers for years to come.

7.1 Background of lump-sum taxation

Lump-sum taxation has traditionally benefited foreigners who were willing to settle down in Switzerland without pursuing a professional activity. Swiss cantons have been offering lump-sum tax legislation to foreigners since the 19th century. Lump-sum taxation has the advantage of being a simple and very competitive mode of taxation for individuals who meet certain requirements.

Currently, lump-sum taxation is available in almost the entire country, except in the cantons of Zurich, Schaffhausen, Appenzell-Ausserrhoden, Basel-Stadt, and

Basel-Landschaft. In 2016, 5,046 persons were taxed under the lump-sum laws in Switzerland,[1] most of them in the cantons of Vaud, Valais, and Geneva.

Federal law provides the basic conditions that need to be met by an individual in order to apply for this beneficial tax regime.[2] Lump-sum taxation is available to foreign nationals who have their tax domicile in Switzerland if they are not exercising any professional activity in the country, and if they have not been Swiss tax residents during the preceding 10 years.

7.2 Why lump-sum taxation?

In essence, lump-sum taxation is an alternative and simplified method of determining the taxable income and wealth of foreign nationals who are tax resident in Switzerland and who are not exercising any professional activities in the country. The tax is levied on deemed income (the 'lump sum') derived from the annual cost of living (see section 7.4). As a result, the effective tax burden can be extremely attractive.

The specifics are discussed with the tax authorities of the canton where the applicant wishes to live, prior to relocation. The tax authorities usually expect full disclosure of the taxpayer's worldwide economic situation at this stage. Consequently, the authorities deliver a legally binding tax ruling to the taxpayer that confirms the modalities of taxation. As a positive side effect, the costs of annual tax compliance are generally much more limited than they would be otherwise.

7.3 Who can benefit from lump-sum taxation?

Non-Swiss nationals who are settling in Switzerland for the first time (or after an absence of 10 years) can request to be taxed on a lump-sum basis. The lump-sum tax regime precludes the taxpayer from exercising any professional activity in Switzerland.

This means that any professional activity needs to be physically performed abroad (i.e. no home office, etc.). Private management of one's own personal wealth is permitted. Swiss board memberships may be tolerated to a limited extent, and subject to confirmation by the tax authorities.

In the case of married couples, both spouses need to meet the respective requirements.

1 Press release of the Swiss conference of cantonal finance ministers, 2 June 2017

2 art 6 Federal Tax Harmonization Act (*Bundesgesetz über die Harmonisierung der direkten Steuern der Kantone und Gemeinden, StHG*); art 14 Federal Direct Tax Act (*Bundesgesetz über die direkte Bundessteuer, DBG*)

7.4 How is taxable income established?

As a starting point, taxable income is determined on the basis of the total annual living expenditure (which serves as a 'deemed taxable income') or of a multiple (7×) of the annual rental costs of the taxpayer and his/her dependents. For federal tax purposes, the minimum taxable income must be at least CHF 400,000. For cantonal tax purposes, the tax base may be lower in some instances.

The relevant amount is usually confirmed by way of negotiations with the authorities, on a case-by-case basis. The authorities therefore expect to receive all relevant information on the applicant's personal and financial situation. This information is kept absolutely confidential.

The following is typically part of the qualifying personal living expenditures:

Food and clothing
Housing
Personal staff
Education and culture
Traveling and vacation
Health care
Costs of vehicles (for example, cars, boats, planes) or animals (for example, horses)
Foreign taxes
Other costs

Total = Taxable income (lump sum, taxed at ordinary rates)

Going forward, the tax authorities generally agree to levy taxes on the basis of the established lump sum as long as the taxpayer's general situation does not change.

7.5 Control calculation

Swiss laws require that the taxable income based on annual expenditure (see section 7.4) be at least as high as the sum of the individual's income sourced in Switzerland. For this purpose, a parallel 'control calculation' must be made. The control calculation especially includes income from Swiss real estate and other assets located in Switzerland (including financial assets), Swiss intellectual property, and Swiss pensions. Income from foreign sources that benefits from double taxation treaties concluded by Switzerland is also included.

There is no capital gains tax on shares or other securities.[3] Therefore, as an example, a gain (or a loss) derived from the sale of shares in a company is tax free, and thus not relevant (and is not taken into account in the control calculation). Capital gains derived from the sale of Swiss real estate will, however, be subject to income tax.

If the income under the control calculation is higher than the lump sum determined based on annual expenditures, the former will be the basis for income tax.

7.6 Double taxation treaties

Certain double taxation treaties concluded by Switzerland provide specific additional requirements for lump-sum taxation. Currently these countries are: Austria, Belgium, Canada, France, Germany, Italy, Norway, and the US.

In essence, individuals taxed on a lump-sum basis need to include the income from these countries in their Swiss tax base in order to benefit from treaty benefits ('modified lump-sum taxation').[4]

7.7 What are the other Swiss taxes due by individuals who are subject to lump-sum taxation?

Wealth tax

In addition to income tax, there is a wealth tax payable in every canton (the tax basis is also determined on a lump-sum basis).[5] The cantons follow varying approaches to determine the wealth tax base in the case of lump-sum taxation; a frequently used method is to multiply the taxable income (see section 7.4) by 20. Thus if a person subject to lump-sum taxation has a taxable income of CHF 1 million, the taxable wealth will amount to CHF 20 million.

Withholding tax

Dividends paid by a Swiss company are subject to Swiss withholding tax (WHT rate of 35%). Swiss tax residents (including persons who are taxed on a lump-sum basis) are entitled to a refund or credit of the WHT against their Swiss income taxes.[6]

---

3 see, for example, art 16(3) DBG

4 see the residence article of these treaties

5 see art 6(5) and 13 et seq StHG

6 art 22 Federal Withholding Tax Act (*Bundesgesetz über die Verrechnungssteuer, VStG*)

Real estate capital gains tax

Gains derived from the sale of Swiss real estate are subject to a separate real estate capital gains tax.[7]

Social security

Being resident in Switzerland, the applicant will also be subject to the Swiss social security system and will therefore be liable to pay social security contributions (and will need private health insurance coverage). The social security contributions payable by individuals who are on lump-sum tax depend on the size of their wealth (the maximum amount is currently roughly CHF 24,000 per year and per person).

Gift and inheritance tax

Gift and inheritance taxes are levied only by the cantons. Being taxed on a lump-sum basis does not in principle exempt an individual from gift and inheritance tax. Schwyz and Obwalden have, however, abolished them altogether, while Lucerne only levies an inheritance tax.

Most cantons have also abolished gift and inheritance tax on transfers between spouses, and to direct descendants. As such, gift and inheritance tax are usually not of major concern to families. The taxation of other transfers depends on the degree of the family relationship and may be subject to higher gift and inheritance tax. Transfers made to charities are tax exempt.

In Geneva, a person who is or has been subject to lump-sum taxation in the three years prior to the gift or inheritance being received will be subject to gift or inheritance tax, even if the beneficiary is a child or the spouse.[8]

Value-added tax

Switzerland has a very low standard value-added tax (VAT) rate of 7.7% as of 1 January 2018 (the current VAT rates in the EU range between 17% and 27%).

7.8 Is there a difference between EU and non-EU nationals?

The conditions for non-EU nationals are frequently more restrictive than for EU nationals. The tax authorities expect higher tax revenues where non-EU nationals

---

7 art 12 StHG

8 art 27A (2) Geneva Law on Registration Taxes (*Loi sur les droits d'enregistrement* — LDE); art 6A (2) Geneva Inheritance Tax Act (*Loi sur les droits de succession* — LDS)

are involved in order to satisfy an 'economic or fiscal interest' that also enables the immigration authorities to deliver the relevant immigration permits. For this very reason, lump-sum taxation has frequently been a popular immigration planning tool for citizens from countries that would otherwise need to observe stricter immigration rules into Switzerland.

Example of calculation

Assume Taxpayer T owns worldwide assets of CHF 500 million. His annual income is CHF 20 million. Further assume Canton X has accepted that T's annual cost of living amounts to CHF 1 million. Canton X determines T's taxable wealth by multiplying his taxable income with a factor of 20. Thus T's taxable income will amount to CHF 1 million and his taxable wealth will amount to CHF 20 million. Assume the standard income tax rate in Canton X is 20% (combined federal, cantonal, and communal) and the annual wealth tax rate is 0.5%. T's annual personal taxes will amount to CHF 200,000 (20% of 1 million) plus CHF 100,000 (0.5% of 20 million). In addition, he will also need to pay social security contributions of roughly CHF 24,000 per year. In total, he will be paying CHF 324,000 per year.

7.9 What is the general attitude of the Swiss tax authorities?

The Swiss tax authorities have a sophisticated and advanced tax ruling practice that has been in place for many decades. The relationship between taxpayers, tax advisors, and tax authorities is generally characterized by a culture of discussion and mutual trust, as well as predictability and stability.

The tax authorities consider taxpayers as their clients. They are well aware of the importance of being economically attractive and of being welcoming to potential taxpayers. As a consequence, it is common practice to approach the tax authorities in the context of major transactions, or prior to the implementation of wealth planning instruments (be it through gifts, the settlement of trusts, the establishment of foundations, etc.). The ruling system is also available to individuals who are taxed on a lump-sum basis.

7.10 What is the procedure to request lump-sum taxation?

Provide information to the tax authorities regarding:

- Personal and family situation (sometimes required: extract from police records at current domicile)
- Financial information: types of income, movable and immovable property, trusts, worldwide costs of living, etc.
- Written and signed confirmation:
  - That the applicant has never been a Swiss tax resident
  - That he/she will not be carrying out any professional activity in Switzerland
  - That he/she is not a Swiss national

Taxation

Submission of a tax ruling request (approximately three to four weeks) determining the taxable income and taxable wealth.

After approval of the ruling, there must be the submission of an immigration permit request (approximately one month) with migration authorities.

Lump-sum taxation is a simple and very competitive taxation option available to individuals in most cantons in Switzerland. It is just one of the attractive taxation regimes that continues to draw wealthy foreign nationals to the country.

About the author

ROBERT DESAX is an attorney and a certified tax expert at the Swiss law firm Walder Wyss. He regularly advises corporate and private clients on cross-border implications of international taxation, especially on the application of double taxation treaties, on issues in connection with the refund of Swiss withholding taxes in international structures, on the Swiss tax treatment of trusts, as well as on the redomiciliation of individuals and businesses to Switzerland. He also frequently represents clients in controversial tax matters, for example, in the areas of inheritance and gift taxes, real estate capital gains tax, or withholding tax.

8 Leaving Germany: The Tax Impact

Dr. Wolf Wassermeyer, Flick Gocke Schaumburg

Taxation

Individuals have many different reasons for moving their tax domicile away from Germany. Their motivation is regularly based on economic, familial, or other personal criteria. Tax aspects also frequently play a substantial, or at least a secondary, role in a move abroad, depending on the individual case.

8.1 Tax motivations for moving to Switzerland

Experience has shown that, up to 2002, if German residents left the country for tax purposes, it was chiefly income tax related factors that prompted their move abroad. After 2002, the introduction of the half-income approach, and the lowering of German income-tax rates, caused a shift in focus in people's motives for moving abroad, from income tax to inheritance tax. Most Swiss cantons do not levy gift or inheritance tax on transfers to spouses or offspring, and Switzerland offers many incentives for newcomers by allowing input tax to be credited under flat-rate income taxation. As a result, Switzerland has long been a popular country for German taxpayers to migrate to.

As a general rule, when relocating, the material tax issues arise in Germany, and not in the destination country. To achieve a tax effect, the tax nexi for German income tax (and/or inheritance tax) liability have to be avoided if possible.

8.2 Income tax issues involved in moving abroad

To fully or partly avoid the income tax consequences of a move from Germany, the first points to address are the prerequisites of the various forms of German income tax liability. This section covers the prerequisites for optimizing the income tax impact of moving away from Germany. Exit taxation is depicted as a particular legal consequence under s 6 of the German Foreign Tax Act (*Außensteuergesetz* — AStG).

German income-tax liability

Like most countries, Germany distinguishes between unlimited and limited income tax liability. Residents moving abroad are also subject to 'extended limited income tax liability' under certain circumstances.

Unlimited tax liability

If an individual's income tax liability in Germany is unlimited, Germany in principle taxes him/her on worldwide income. Germany's right to tax an individual may potentially be restricted by an applicable double taxation treaty (DTT). Unlimited tax liability arises under German income tax law if the person in question has a domicile within the meaning of s 8 of the German General Tax Code (*Abgabenordnung* — AO), or his/her habitual abode within the meaning of s 9 of the AO in Germany.[1]

Limited tax liability

If an individual maintains neither a domicile within the meaning of s 8 of the AO, nor his/her habitual abode within the meaning of s 9 of the AO in Germany, this person is subject to limited tax liability.[2] The legal consequence is that this individual is subject to German taxation only under the categories of German-sourced income listed in s 49(1) of the EStG. Germany's right to taxation may also become restricted by an applicable DTT.

Extended limited tax liability

If an individual ceases to be subject to unlimited German tax liability, he/she will become subject to extended limited tax liability under s 2 of the AStG under the following prerequisites:

1 s 1(1) sentence 1 of the German Income Tax Act (*Einkommensteuergesetz* — EStG)
2 s 1(4) EStG

- The emigrant was, as a German, subject to at least five years' unlimited tax liability in the previous 10 years before such liability ended
- The emigrant will become resident in a low tax jurisdiction, or in no state, and does not pay income tax there. The income tax corresponds to at least two thirds of a German tax that would be levied if unlimited tax liability is assumed to exist. The German tax authorities will always assume that low taxation occurs in Switzerland due to the system of allowing input tax to be credited against the Swiss flat-rate taxation regime
- The emigrant still has business interests in Germany, in the form of an interest exceeding 25% in a German partnership or corporation, non-foreign income exceeding EUR 52,000, or non-foreign assets exceeding EUR 154,000

The legal consequence of extended limited tax liability is that the list of taxable income is extended for the year of departure, and the 10 following years for all non-foreign income under s 34c(1) of the EStG. Consequently, Germany's right to tax also encompasses, for example, interest owed by Germans that would not be included in limited tax liability. Germany's right to taxation can in principle continue to be restricted by an applicable DTT. Furthermore, under s 50a of the EStG, final withholding tax (*Abgeltungsteuer*) does not apply. Moreover, taxable income is subject to the progression clause, meaning that the individual is required to report his/her worldwide income during extended tax liability. He/she can regularly avoid the consequences of extended limited income tax liability by restructuring his/her assets.

Prerequisites for a tax-optimized move abroad

Tax-wise, two effective options exist in principle for moving from Germany to Switzerland. These solutions restrict German income tax liability, and optimize the tax applicable to the move abroad. Either the individual seeks to avoid the income tax nexi for German income tax liability — in particular, German unlimited income tax liability (Option 1), or the individual establishes a dual domicile and comes under the protection of the DTT/Switzerland by shifting the center of his/her vital interests to Switzerland (Option 2).

Option 1: Elimination of domestic nexi

Under Option 1, the emigrant gives up his/her domicile and habitual abode in Germany, and thus ends his/her unlimited German tax liability. If necessary, he/she also seeks to avoid tax nexi for (extended) limited income tax liability.

(1) Giving up one's German domicile

A person's domicile is where he/she maintains a dwelling under circumstances that lead to the conclusion that he/she will keep and use the dwelling.[3] To establish unlimited tax liability in the domestic country on the basis of a domicile, it is of significance whether the taxpayer has further domiciles at home or abroad,[4] or where the center of his/her vital interests is situated.[5] A dwelling in this sense encompasses all premises that are suited for living,[6] such as a furnished room, a second residence, a hunting lodge,[7] or holiday home.[8] A hotel room permanently at the individual's disposal is also sufficient. It is immaterial for tax purposes under s 8 of the AO whether a principal or secondary domicile is involved.[9] 'Maintaining' a dwelling presupposes that the person in question may use the dwelling at will. The actual right of use is crucial;[10] it is therefore not absolutely decisive who the legal tenant or owner of the dwelling is. As part of an overall evaluation, all the actual circumstances[11] that show that the dwelling serves as a lodging, that it is used constantly or at least regularly and habitually and is not designed solely for

3 s 8 AO
4 Federal Tax Court of 19 March 2002, BFH/NV 2002, 1411, 1412; Gersch in: Klein, AO, § 8 recitals 2 and 5; Heinicke in: Schmidt, EStG, § 1 recital 20, Kruse in: Kruse, Tipke AO/FGO, § 8 AO recital 4 with further references
5 Federal Tax Court of 24 January 2001, BFH/NV 2001, 1402, 1403; of 19 March 2002, BFH/NV 2002, 1411, 1412; Heinicke in: Schmidt, EStG, § 1 recital 20
6 AEAO recital 3; Heinicke in: Schmidt, EStG, § 1 recital 21; Birk in: Hepp,Hübschmann,Spitaler, AO/FGO, § 8 AO recital 19 et seq with further references
7 RFH of 3 April 1941, RStBI. 1941, 290
8 Heinicke in: Schmidt, EStG, § 1 recital 21; Gersch in: Klein, AO, § 8 recital 2 Kruse in: Kruse, Tipke, AO/FGO, § 8 AO recitals 5 and 8; Birk in: Hepp,Hübschmann,Spitaler, AO/FGO, § 8 AO recitals 23 and 26 with further references
9 Federal Tax Court of 24 January 2001, I R 100/99, BFH/NV 2001, 1402; Cologne Tax Court of 27 June 2002, 10 K 6348/97, EFG 2002, 1198
10 Federal Tax Court of 23 November II R 1988, 139/87, Federal Tax Gazette Part II 1989, 182, 183; Federal Tax Court of 12 January 2001, VI R 64/98 BFH/NV 2001, 1231, 1232; AEAO recital 4; Heinicke in: Schmidt, EStG, § 1 recital 22; Kruse in: Kruse, Tipke, AO/FGO, § 8 AO recitals 6; Birk in: Hepp,Hübschmann,Spitaler, AO/FGO, § 8 AO recital 28
11 Federal Tax Court of 19 March 1997, I R 69/96, Federal Tax Gazette Part II 1997, 447, 448; Federal Tax Court of 19 March 2002, I R 15/01, BFH/NV 2002, 1411, 1412; Kruse in: Kruse, Tipke, AO/FGO, § 8 AO recitals 9; Gersch in: Klein, AO, 9th ed 2006, § 8 recital 4

the purposes of a temporary residence,[12] must also be taken into account. Having the intention to establish a domicile is not required,[13] nor is the permanent use of the dwelling,[14] or a stay for a specific minimum period.[15] Short stays in Germany for holiday and recreational purposes do not create a domicile per se[16] but can be sufficient for the tax authorities to assume that a dwelling (which will be retained) exists before the individual moves abroad.[17] On the other hand, registering with the police in a specific place serves as an indicator[18] of a domicile at most.[19]

It should be noted that the tax authorities will presume that spouses have a joint family domicile.[20] Accordingly, they will proceed on the assumption that the one spouse also uses the dwelling in which his/her family lives, and will therefore have a domicile there as well.[21] It is true that this assumption can be refuted, but only by proof in the individual case that the spouse is not expected to return to the joint domicile.[22] It will hardly be possible, or only extremely difficult, to furnish such proof as long as one spouse continues to maintain a domicile in Germany, and is not divorced or proven to be permanently separated from the spouse who emigrated. Proving this is all the more difficult if offspring continue to maintain a domicile in Germany.

If the individual wishes to avoid a German domicile with legal certainty, all dwellings actually used in Germany should be given up, and ideally the facts should be substantiated by terminating a tenancy agreement, or selling the dwelling to a third party.

12 Heinicke in: Schmidt, EStG, § 1 recital 23. Similarly Gersch in: Klein, AO, § 8 recital 4
13 AEAO recital 2 sentence 1, Kruse in: Kruse, Tipke, AO/FGO, § 8 dAO recital 2; Heinicke in: Schmidt, EStG, § 1 recital 21
14 Heinicke in: Schmidt, EStG, § 1 recital 23; Federal Tax Court of 19 March 2002, I R 15/01, BFH/NV 2002, 1411, 1412
15 Federal Tax Court of 12 January 2001, VI R 64/98, BFH/NV 2001, 1231, 1232
16 Federal Tax Court of 6 March 1968; I 38/65, Federal Tax Gazette Part II 1968, 439 (440)
17 Heinicke in: Schmidt, EStG, § 1 recital 23; Federal Tax Court of 12 January 2001, VI R 64/98, BFH/NV 2001, 1231, 1232; Tax Court of Lower Saxony of 9 September 2004, file no 10 V 302/04 (not published)
18 View taken by the tax authorities, see AEAO recital 2 sentence 3
19 Federal Tax Court of 14 November 1969, III R 95/68, Federal Tax Gazette Part II 1970, 153, 155; Federal Tax Court of 12 April 1978, I R 136/77, Federal Tax Gazette Part II 1978, 494, 495; Gersch in: Klein, AO, § 8 recital 5; Heinicke in: Schmidt, EStG, § 1 recital 23
20 Federal Tax Court of 17 May 1995, I R 8/94, Federal Tax Gazette Part II 1996, 2
21 St Rspr (established case law); Federal Tax Court of 17 May 1995, I R 8/94, Federal Tax Gazette Part II 1996, 2 with further references
22 Federal Tax Court of 29 October 1959, IV129/58 S, Federal Tax Gazette Part III 1960, 61

Taxation

(2) Terminating habitual abode

To avoid German unlimited income tax liability, the emigrant must give up not only his German domicile, but also his/her habitual abode in Germany. Habitual abode exists if a person stays in Germany under circumstances that lead to the conclusion that the person does not only temporarily stay at the location.[23] In each individual case the objective circumstances are decisive; the personal wish of the individual is not relevant, even if it contradicts the actual circumstances.[24] 'Staying' or 'spending time' presupposes physical presence in Germany.[25] If the stay continues for a considerable length of time it can no longer be considered temporary; it is worth noting that the law does not specify any minimum period. Habitual abode is always assumed for an ongoing stay exceeding six months.[26] In specific cases, however, the duration of a stay can also be (substantially) less than six months. It is also not necessary in a particular case for the stay to take place without interruption. In contrast, stays for visiting, recreational, spa, or similar personal purposes are not harmful.

An individual gives up his/her habitual abode within the meaning of s 9 sentence 1 of the AO if he/she ceases to stay at the place or in the region, and the external circumstances do not create the impression that he/she will return, and continue to stay there. Following s 9 sentence 2 of the AO, this can be presumed if the person stays abroad for more than six months.[27] This is, however, refuted if, despite the absence, the objective circumstances indicate that the individual will return and continue to stay at the place or in the region.[28] In any case, to the extent that the person establishes his/her habitual abode abroad, the German habitual abode must be given up, because establishing a new habitual abode means that the existing one is given up.[29]

Spouses establish their habitual abode independently of each other.[30] Therefore, crediting the spouse's habitual abode is — unlike in the case of the domicile (see above) — not an option.

One further criterion for the existence of a habitual abode in Germany, is if the individual spends three to four days a week pursuing his/her profession in Germany.

---

23 s 9 AO

24 Stapperfend, in: Herrmann, Heuer, Raupach, EStG, § 1 recital 76 with further references

25 Kruse, in: Kruse, Tipke, AO/FGO, § 9 AO recital 4

26 s 9 sentence 2 AO

27 Federal Tax Court of 27 July 1962, VI 156/59, Federal Tax Gazette Part III 1962, 429; Kruse, in: Kruse, Tipke, AO/FGO, § 9 AO recital 16; Stapperfend, in: Herrmann, Heuer, Raupach, EStG/dKStG, § 1 EStG recital 83

28 Stapperfend, in: Herrmann, Heuer, Raupach, EStG/KStG, § 1 EStG recital 83 with reference to the Tax Court of Baden-Württemberg of 23 September 1975, EFG 1976, 13

29 Federal Tax Court of 27 April 2005, I R 112/04, BFH/NV 2005, 1756

30 Federal Tax Court of 14 November 1969, III R 95/68, Federal Tax Gazette Part II 1970, 153

It is immaterial whether, on the remaining week days, the individual stays at the foreign family domicile that forms the center of his/her vital interests.[31]

(3) Legal consequences of a move abroad

If the emigrant has given up his/her domicile and habitual abode in Germany, he/she has effectively moved abroad. In other words, the individual ceases to be subject to unlimited income-tax liability in Germany, and must pay tax only on certain German-sourced income, i.e. he/she is subject to German (extended) limited tax liability. If he/she moves to Switzerland, Germany's right to tax this income may also be restricted by the applicable DTT/Switzerland. It may be advisable to avoid leaving any sources of income in Germany by restructuring German assets into foreign assets. Consequently, the restriction on Germany's right to taxation becomes even further-reaching.

Option 2: Triggering the protection afforded by the DTT/Switzerland (dual domicile)

Tax-wise, an effective move to Switzerland can, in theory, also be achieved by retaining a German domicile and German unlimited income tax liability, but also becoming a Swiss resident under treaty law and relocating one's permanent home (*Wohnstätte*), and center of vital interests to Switzerland. This would restrict Germany's right to tax certain types of German-sourced income specified in the DTT/Switzerland. However, this second option in relation to Switzerland is virtually impossible to apply in practice, for the following reasons.

(1) No treaty protection under art 4(6) DTT/Switzerland

This second option would not be feasible if the emigrant pays Swiss flat-rate tax in Switzerland on German-sourced income. This would have the legal consequence that, under art 4(6) DTT/Switzerland, the emigrant is not protected by treaty law, which is necessary for an effective move abroad as per Option 2.

(2) Extended unlimited liability under art 4(3) DTT/Switzerland

Additionally, Germany may continue to tax the emigrant's worldwide income under art 4(3) DTT/Switzerland — in simplified terms — by crediting Swiss tax if the emigrant maintains a permanent home in Germany.

31 Federal Tax Court of 22 June 2011, BFH/NV 2011, 2001 et seqq

The term 'home' (*Wohnstätte*) should not objectively differ from domicile (*Wohnsitz*), the term used in domestic law (see above). Unlike the domicile, the permanent home must be used regularly, as the term permanent (*ständig*) indicates. A permanent home in this sense, is any premises frequented in a way that represents a point of contact integrated into the taxpayer's general rhythm of life and not simply a place visited on occasion. The Federal Tax Court determined that a domicile constitutes a permanent home in principle, if it is used on 50 days a year.[32] However, it cannot be inferred according to the Federal Tax Court that use of the domicile of less than 50 days a year does not create a permanent home. Still, the Court went on to rule that no permanent home exists if the domicile is used only a few days per year due to business activity. A permanent home does not include dwellings or premises that, by their character and location, serve only recreational, spa, study or sports purposes, and are proven to be used only on occasion and not for the purposes of pursuing business or professional interests.[33]

If the emigrant moves from Germany to Switzerland according to Option 2, he/she should be permitted to retain a domicile in Germany that is not classified as a permanent home. This is possible only in rare cases, and can be substantiated in these rare cases only with great difficulty. The only conceivable exception is a holiday home that is occasionally used. For this reason, Option 2 is usually impractical.

(3) Legal consequences of the move abroad under Option 2

If the emigrant has established a permanent home in Switzerland (retaining merely a domicile in Germany that does not constitute a permanent home), and he/she has no German-sourced income that is subject to Swiss flat-rate taxation, the emigrant has thus become a Swiss resident under treaty law. The legal consequence is that Germany may tax only the types of German-sourced income listed under arts 6 to 22 DTT/Switzerland. It may be advisable to avoid any German-sourced income by restructuring German assets into foreign assets. As a consequence, the restriction on Germany's right to taxation would become even further-reaching.

Specific legal consequence: Exit taxation under s 6 of the AStG

If an emigrant holds at least 1% of the shares of a German or foreign corporation as personal assets, he/she, in principle, triggers 'exit taxation' under s 6 of the AStG, which can be deferred for five or possibly 10 years in exchange for security.

32 Federal Tax Court of 5 June 2007, Federal Tax Gazette Part II 2007, 812

33 Minutes of the negotiations on DTT/Switzerland 1971 of 18 June 1971, for arts 4(2) and (3)

The key objective of exit taxation under s 6(1) of StG is to tax hidden reserves embedded in shares — from a tax perspective — held privately in German or foreign corporations within the meaning of s 17 of the EStG, if these hidden reserves are withdrawn from the German tax net by an event with a foreign nexus. 'Shares in corporations' means not only stocks or business shares, but also jouissance certificates or similar interests and claims to such interests.[34] The shareholder within the meaning of s 17 of the EStG is the beneficial owner of the shares, in accordance with s 39 of the AO. In principle, s 6 of the AStG provides for a deemed capital gain if the emigrant ceased to be subject to unlimited tax liability in Germany, or the applicable DTT deprives Germany of its right to tax these shares because the taxpayer has shifted the center of his/her vital interests. The same applies in principle if the taxpayer gives or leaves the shares to a recipient who is resident abroad.[35]

In these cases, the deemed capital gain, i.e. the difference between the market value and the historical acquisition costs of the shares, must in principle be taxed in Germany at a rate of up to about 28.5% (taxation in accordance with the 'partial-income approach').

If German exit taxation is applied in principle, the question arises of whether and how it can be avoided.[36] Various structuring approaches are available to avoid exit taxation, but their feasibility always has to be reviewed on a case-by-case basis.

(1) Interest-free deferral of payment under s 6(5) of the AStG

A national of an EU member state is permitted to apply for long-term interest-free deferral of exit taxation without providing any security, if he/she moves to a member state of the EU or the European Economic Area (EEA), and is subject to tax liability similar to German income taxation.[37] These criteria do not exist per se if a taxpayer moves to Switzerland, because Switzerland is a member of neither the EU nor the EEA. However, Switzerland entered into an agreement on the free movement of persons, under which freedom of establishment and the free movement of capital, also apply in relation to Switzerland. As the introduction of the major information clause under treaty law also guarantees sufficient exchange of information with Switzerland within the meaning of s 6(5) sentence 2 of the AStG, the interest-free deferral of payment should also be applicable after moving to Switzerland.[38] However, it is unlikely that the tax authorities will accept this interpretation.

34 s 17(1) sentence 3 EStG
35 s 6(1) sentence 2 no 1 AStG
36 Häck, in: Haase, AStG/DBA, § 6 AStG recital 263 et seqq
37 s 6(5) AStG
38 Also argued thus in: Häck, IStR 2011, 797

(2) Deferral of payment under s 6(3) of the AStG

German exit taxation can be deferred temporarily for five years, if the emigrant intends to return to Germany within the five-year time limit.[39] This limit can be extended on condition that the taxpayer has professional reasons for his/her absence and still intends to return. This deferral of payment is interest-free, and in principle not subject to the provision of security. If the emigrant sells the interest during his/her absence or does not return to Germany within the time limit, the deferral is revoked and the exit tax falls due. If the emigrant returns to Germany within the time limit, the exit tax ceases to apply, and the relevant tax notice must be amended.

(3) Flat-rate taxation

German exit tax on holdings in corporations can also be avoided by making German-sourced income subject to flat-rate taxation in Switzerland. In this case, art 4(6) of the DTT/Switzerland does not apply. If the emigrant also retains a (secondary) domicile in Germany, he/she would not give up his/her unlimited tax liability in Germany, thus avoiding the legal consequences of exit taxation. However, this does not change the emigrant's tax position in Germany, which is why this variant is not particularly attractive as a rule.

(4) Conversion into a partnership

One further way to avoid German exit taxation can be to convert a corporation into a partnership. Under ss 9 in conjunction with 3 et seqq of the German Reorganization Tax Act (*Umwandlungssteuergesetz* — UmwStG), a change of legal form would in principle be tax neutral in Germany. Corresponding regulations exist in all the other EU member states. It needs to be borne in mind that a change of legal form can have secondary tax consequences, such as a taxable take-over profit, a taxable deemed distribution of retained earnings, the elimination of losses carried forward, and acquisition costs.

(5) Contribution to a trading partnership

The final option for avoiding exit taxation in some cases is to make a gratuitous contribution to a German trading partnership, which is a tax neutral transaction.

39 s 6(3) AStG

In principle, a contribution can be made without triggering tax, if done so without consideration.[40] Exit taxation applies only if the interest is held privately by the emigrant, which is not the case with a contribution to a trading partnership. It is possible that the emigrant's move could invoke a departure from the German tax net under s 4(1) sentence 3 of the EStG if Germany's right to tax the holdings contributed to a corporation is impaired. A departure from the German tax net would cause the hidden reserves of the holdings in the corporation to be taxed in Germany (ultimately like exit taxation). A departure from the German tax net and German exit taxation can be avoided with legal certainty[41] if a functional connection exists between the activity performed by the German partnership and the activity performed by the corporation. Then the holding must be attributed to a German permanent establishment under treaty law, in accordance with arts 10(5), art 13(2) of the DTT/Switzerland, with Germany retaining its right to tax the capital gains. Exit taxation under a 6(1) of the AStG, or leaving the tax net under s 4(1) sentence 3 of the EStG does not apply in these cases.

8.3 Inheritance tax issues involved in moving abroad

To fully or partly avoid the legal consequences of a move abroad in terms of gift and inheritance tax in Germany, the first points to address are the prerequisites of the various forms of German income tax liability (for details, see section 8.2). These indicate the prerequisites for a tax-optimized move from Germany.

German inheritance tax liability

Germany distinguishes between unlimited and limited income tax liability. Extended unlimited and extended limited tax liability also exist.

Unlimited tax liability

A taxpayer is subject to German inheritance or gift tax liability, if either the person with dispositional rights (i.e. the deceased or the donor), or the beneficiary in Germany (as is the case with income tax), has a domicile within the meaning of s 8 of the AO, or a habitual abode within the meaning of s 9 of the AO. The legal consequence is that all the taxpayer's worldwide assets transferred gratuitously are liable to inheritance or gift tax in Germany.

40 Federal Ministry of Finance guidance of 7 July 2011, Federal Tax Gazette 2011 Part I, 713 annotation II with further references

41 Federal Tax Court judgment of 24 August 2011, I R 46/10; with further references

Extended unlimited tax liability

If the person with dispositional rights or the beneficiary is a German national, he/she is also subject to 'extended unlimited inheritance or gift tax liability' in Germany for five years after giving up a domicile or a habitual abode. The legal consequence is that all the taxpayer's worldwide assets transferred gratuitously remain liable to inheritance or gift tax in Germany during the subsequent five-year period mentioned above.

Limited tax liability

If the person with dispositional rights (the deceased or donor), or the beneficiary has a domicile within the meaning of s 8 of the OA, or a habitual abode within the meaning of s 9 of the AO in Germany, only the gratuitous transfers via the domestic assets held in Germany within the meaning of s 121 of the German Valuation Act (*Bewertungsgesetz* — BewG) are subject to German gift or inheritance tax. The main cases of domestic assets to which this applies, are real estate located in Germany, business assets situated in Germany, and directly or indirectly held interests in German corporations of at least 10%.

Extended limited tax liability

If the deceased or a donor were subject to extended limited income tax liability at the time of the gratuitous transfer, extended limited inheritance and gift tax liability applies. Accordingly, all gratuitous transfers of extended domestic assets are taxable in Germany. Extended domestic assets exist if the income from the assets of a person subject to unlimited income tax liability represents non-foreign income within the meaning of s 34c(1) of the EStG. This results, for example, in the gratuitous transfer of debt claims against a German debtor becoming liable to inheritance or gift tax. This definition of assets therefore extends beyond the scope of domestic assets in terms of limited tax liability and applies at most for the year of the move abroad and the 10 following years. Extended limited inheritance and gift tax liability can regularly be avoided by restructuring the assets at the disposal of the potential taxpayer.

Prerequisites for a tax-optimized move abroad

In principle, two methods exist for avoiding German inheritance and gift tax when moving to Switzerland, thus optimizing the impact of inheritance tax when moving abroad.

Option 1: Elimination of all domestic nexi

This method presupposes that unlimited and limited inheritance- and gift-tax liability can be avoided in Germany. On the one hand, this means that both the deceased or donor and the beneficiary have to give up their domicile and habitual abode in Germany. If the prerequisites for extended unlimited tax liability are met, the deceased, donor, and beneficiary must have had neither a domicile nor a habitual abode in Germany for over five years before the transfer in Germany. On the other hand, to avoid German (extended) limited inheritance and gift tax liability, no right of control over (extended) domestic assets may exist. If domestic assets are affected by the envisaged transfers these assets should be converted into foreign assets by restructuring, contribution, or assignment to foreign entities.

Subject to the above prerequisites, a move abroad would be optimized for inheritance tax purposes. The gratuitous transfers would then not be liable to any inheritance or gift tax.

Option 2: Invoking the protection afforded by the DTT/Switzerland (Inheritance Tax)

In theory, German inheritance or gift tax can also be avoided by seeking protection under the DDT/Switzerland (Inheritance Tax). If the deceased or donor is, or was, resident in Switzerland under treaty law at the time of the gratuitous transfer because he/she is or was subject to unlimited tax liability and maintains or maintained his permanent home and center of his vital interests there, Germany's right to taxation will be restricted. In this case, arts 5–8 of the DTT/Switzerland (Inheritance Tax) stipulate that only German real estate, German ships and aircrafts, and German permanent establishments may, in principle, be taxed in Germany. However, this restriction is again limited by art 8(2) of the DTT/Switzerland (Inheritance Tax). As such, Germany retains its right to taxation by crediting any Swiss tax, if the acquirer maintains a permanent home or his/her habitual abode in Germany. The restriction contained in art 8(2) of the DTT/Switzerland (Inheritance Tax) does not apply if the deceased and the acquirer are Swiss citizens at the time of death.

This chapter considered the tax implications of moving from Germany to Switzerland and offers practical advice on how to structure one's fiscal affairs to best gain a tax advantage when relocating.

About the author

DR. WOLF WASSERMEYER has been a lawyer since 1996, a certified tax advisor since 1999, and an an expert advisor on international tax law and partner since 2002. He studied law in Constance and Kiel (1995 Dr. iur.). He is guest lecturer at the *Bundesfinanzakademie* (German Federal Finance Academy) and lecturer at the Fresenius University of Applied Sciences, Munich.

9 The State Pension Scheme

Gertrud E. Bollier, gebo Sozialversicherungen AG

Pension

In Switzerland, social security, i.e. protection against life's major risks (for example illness, accidents, disability, unemployment, old age, death of the family breadwinner) is provided through 10 social insurance schemes.

This chapter provides a brief overview of Swiss social security funds and the Swiss pension system, followed by details of the obligatory payment contributions for employed and non-employed individuals residing in Switzerland.

9.1 Swiss social security

Table 9.1 Social security contributions in Switzerland

SOCIAL SECURITY CONTRIBUTIONS FOR INSURANCE AGAINST MAIN RISKS	
Illnesses	Health insurance, accident insurance for work-related diseases, military insurance
Accidents	Accident insurance or health insurance, military insurance
Disability (incapacity to work)	Disability insurance (*Invalidenversicherung* — IV), supplementary benefits to IV, occupational pension provision, accident, and military insurance
Unemployment	Unemployment insurance
Old age	Old-age and survivors' insurance (*Alters- und Hinterlassenenversicherung* — AHV), supplementary benefits to AHV, occupational pension scheme
The main breadwinner's death	AHV, supplementary benefits for AHV, occupational pension, accident, and military insurance

The list of insurance types does not include those offering income compensation for those providing services, those on maternity leave (*Mutterschaft* – EO) or family benefits, i.e. child benefit. Strictly speaking, military insurance and supplementary benefits to the old-age and survivors' insurance (*Alters- und Hinterlassenenversicherung* – AHV)/Disability insurance (*Invalidenversicherung* – IV) (earners' pensions) are not insurance because they are financed exclusively by taxpayers' money.

In Switzerland, old-age and survivors' insurance was the first compulsory insurance — referred to as compulsory social security. It is this insurance that determines who falls within the Swiss social security system, categorizing who is employed, self-employed, and not employed.

The three-pillar system

In Switzerland social security has developed relatively late and fairly slowly. For the most part, the concept of social security was created after the Second World War, and then continuously expanded according to the needs of the people.

Pension

A milestone in the development of the Swiss pension system which came in 1972, was the incorporation of the so-called 'three-pillar concept' in the Federal Constitution.[1] It was on this concept that the financial security of the Swiss population was based to protect against disability, death and old age. The three pillars refer to state, occupational, and private provision.

First pillar: The state pension scheme

The state pension scheme, in the form of compulsory old-age, survivors' and disability insurance, as well as supplementary benefits (EL), aims to secure one's livelihood. The insurance covers the entire resident population and is primarily managed by the AHV funds. Financing is based on the expenditure apportionment procedure. This means that contributions collected in a certain period are paid back as benefits during that same period. The most important means of financing the scheme are contributions from insured individuals and employers (AHV approximately 70%, IV approximately 50%, EL 0%) as well as taxpayers' money. The obligation to pay contributions is not limited to a certain income level for employed individuals, but is open ended. Non-employed people pay contributions on the basis of their assets and replacement income (pensions, daily allowances, etc.). However, these contributions are capped, however.

1 now art 111 BV

Second pillar: The occupational pension scheme

The occupational pension scheme, together with the benefits of the first pillar, aims to ensure that an individual's accustomed standard of living is maintained. The Federal Act on Occupational Pensions (BVG) is a framework law. In addition to the mandatory regulations regarding the scope of insured earnings and benefits, pension plans — also known as pension funds — may provide for more extensive provisions. The decisive factors are the regulations of the pension fund in question. Only AHV-liable employees whose wages exceed three quarters of the maximum possible AHV retirement pension are compulsorily insured in the occupational pension scheme. Self-employed individuals can take out voluntary insurance. This pillar is primarily paid out via pension funds. These are organizations independent of the employer, usually in the legal form of a foundation. In contrast to AHV/IV and most other social insurance schemes, funding is financed by the capital cover scheme. This means that the capital required for the pension payment of each individual is created in a savings scheme.

Third pillar: Private provision

Private provision ultimately leaves it to the discretion of each individual to supplement the benefits from the first and second pillars with their private savings, home ownership, and life insurance, in accordance with their individual wishes and needs. The Swiss Confederation and the cantons have the task of supporting private provision with funds from property ownership and fiscal policy (tied provision pillar 3a). Individual needs can be covered freely at any time in the free pension plan (pillar 3b), but restrictive regulations apply to the tied pension plan (pillar 3a) in the form of tax benefits. For example, the tied pension plan is only open to employees who are subject to AHV contributions. Their annual contributions are limited and may be drawn no earlier than five years before reaching the normal AHV retirement age. In the event of death, a legal order of succession must also be observed.

Health insurance

In most industrialized countries social health insurance is financed as a percentage of wages, and non-employed family members are also insured. This is not the case in Switzerland, where a per capita reward system applies. This means that every person must take out compulsory basic health insurance with a recognized insurance provider within three months of taking up residence in Switzerland. Premiums vary depending on the health insurer, the type of insurance chosen, and the place of residence of the individual.

In Switzerland, there is no compulsory sickness daily benefits insurance (except for a collective agreement). As a result, accidents that take place outside of working hours involving employees who work at least eight hours a week for a single employer, and self-employed people with voluntary insurance, are covered by their accident insurance plans.

9.2 Employed persons' contributions to state benefits

Employed individuals are obliged to pay contributions on 1 January from the age of 17 until the end of the month in which they reach 65 years of age. For women, the pension age is set at 64 years. Whoever continues to work beyond this period, must continue to pay contributions from an AHV-liable income exceeding CHF 1,400 per month. These contributions are, however, no longer pension forming. They are solidarity contributions, i.e. a type of social tax. In the unemployment insurance scheme, employed individuals of retirement age are not covered by insurance cover, and are not obligated to pay contributions.

Self-employed or non-self-employed

A distinction must be made between self-employed and non-self-employed persons to establish who is obliged to pay contributions. For activities carried out in Switzerland, the AHV decides on the relevant status for all social security funds. Self-employed persons are those who have their own business and operate in their own name for their own account, using their own funds for the most part. In Switzerland, unlike in neighboring countries, the managing directors of a limited liability company (GmbH), foundations or associations, as well as members of a board of directors, are considered to be non-self-employed.

It should be noted that:

- Not every contract carried out by a person recognized as self-employed is considered to be a self-employed activity. Each individual contract is reviewed on a case-by-case basis. Freelancers are generally regarded as non-self-employed

- The employer is liable to AHV compensation for the employer's and employee's share of the income from non-self-employed earnings
- In financially significant cases, the client can have the relevant AHV compensation fund clarify in advance whether the freelancer is considered to be self-employed. To do this, the query must be presented in writing with the invoice of the freelancer, specifying his/her self-employed status
- Employed individuals are obligated to contribute to unemployment insurance, the family allowance scheme, accident insurance and, if they earn a certain amount of money, an occupational pension scheme
- Self-employed people are not obligated to have this insurance cover, but they must pay full AHV/IV/EO contributions as well as those of the family compensation fund

Obligatory contributions for self-employed individuals

Self-employed persons are subject to the AHV compensation fund responsible for them, on the basis of their net income from self-employment according to direct federal tax. The cantonal AHV compensation fund, often called the Social Insurance Institution (SVA) is responsible for this at the company's registered office. If the person concerned is a member of a professional association with its own AHV compensation fund, the association is responsible (for example, Medisuisse for doctors, Baumeister for the construction industry, Arbeitgeber Basel for companies in the Basel region, Zürcher Arbeitgeber for companies in the Zürich region, etc.). The list of AHV compensation funds can be found at *ahv-iv.ch*.

The AHV compensation fund collects contributions for AHV, disability insurance, and the income compensation scheme (AHV/IV/EO). For annual incomes of CHF 56,400 and above, this is 9.65%. For lower incomes, a declining contribution scale is applied. The net income from self-employment is determined by deducting the necessary costs of production from the gross income. Any AHV/IV/EO contributions deducted in the tax return for the self-employed person must be offset again.

Every year, the AHV sets contributions in accordance with the federal and cantonal tax authorities. The contribution year is the calendar year. The last day of the fiscal year is the cut-off date for the valuation of equity invested in a company. As a rule, contributions are made on a quarterly basis. The contribution amount is determined by the AHV compensation fund by assessing the expected income for the following year, based on the income of the last year. If it becomes apparent during or after the end of the contribution year that income differs significantly from the expected income the compensation fund adjusts the contribution amount.

- When a person commences self-employment, the AHV compensation fund collects the AHV/IV/EO contributions on the basis of the self-reported information provided by the individual. The AHV compensation fund receives the necessary data from the cantonal tax office to collect the contributions
- The information provided by the cantonal tax authorities is binding. Any wrong decisions must be appealed by contacting the tax authorities within the time limit for objections. Only in the case of an official complaint against the AHV contribution decision will it be checked if the compensation fund has correctly assessed the values submitted by the tax authority
- In accordance with the federal and cantonal tax authorities, the AHV sets contributions once a year. The last day of the fiscal year is the cut-off date for the valuation of equity invested in a company

Table 9.2 Contributions for self-employed individuals

SELF-EMPLOYED INDIVIDUALS OBLIGED TO PAY CONTRIBUTIONS **From self-employed net income based on direct federal tax payments** **(contribution payment via compensation fund)**	
7.8% 1.4% 0.45%	AHV IV EO
9.65%	**Total annual income starting from CHF 56,400** With a decreasing scale going down to 5.196%, with a minimum of CHF 487 per year
+ maximum 0.5% + from 2013 approx. 2%	Administrative expenses Family allowances

The self-employed are, like employees and certain groups of non-employed individuals, subject to the Federal Act on Family Allowances (FamZG). The corresponding contributions for self-employed people are capped at an annual income of CHF 148,200 (see Table 9.3 for administrative expenses). Self-employed individuals are free to take out a pension fund (*Pensionskasse* — BVG) and accident insurance. Self-employed individuals have no access to unemployment insurance.

Obligatory contributions for non-self-employed individuals

Non-self-employed persons are obligatory members of the AHV compensation fund and the pension fund (*Pensionskasse*) to which the employer is affiliated. The employer deducts his/her share of social security contributions from his/her salary and transfers this, together with other contributions, to the relevant social insurers.

The decisive salary is the basis for determining the contribution to be paid by the non-self-employed person (usually an employee). The decisive salary is defined as any remuneration for work performed in an employed position for a certain or indefinite period of time, which is not reimbursed for expenses.[2] The decisive salary in accordance with the AHV Act is the starting point for the contribution obligation of the other social insurers.

Table 9.3 Contributions for non-self-employed individuals

OBLIGATORY CONTRIBUTIONS FOR NON-SELF-EMPLOYED INDIVIDUALS EMPLOYERS AND EMPLOYEES EACH PAY HALF OF THE SALARY (CONTRIBUTIONS BY COMPENSATION FUND IS ENTIRELY THE EMPLOYER'S DECISION)		
Employee %	**Social security/insurance**	**Employer %**
4.2	**AHV**	4.2
0.7	**IV**	0.7
0.225	**EO**	0.225
5.125	**AHV/IV/EO**	5.125
1.1 (+)	**ALV**	1.1 (+)
–	Family allowances	2.0 ca.
–	Administrative expenses	0.3 ca.
6.225 + NBUV/BVG	**Total**	**8.525** + BUV/BVG

The AHV/IV/EO contribution amount is open-ended. Unemployment insurance (*Arbeitslosenversicherung* — ALV) covers annual wages of up to CHF 148,200 with contributions of 1.1% each. For annual income from CHF 148,201, an additional 0.5% for each type of contribution is charged to cover the deficit in the ALV compensation fund.

2 *MFact/Merkblätter & Formulare/Beiträge, 2.01 — Abs 10–13, ahv-iv.ch*

Each employer must join a family compensation fund for his or her staff, and pay appropriate contributions on the relevant salary. These vary between 1.2% and 3.6% (cantonal family compensation funds) depending on the local benefits on offer.

The AHV compensation fund charges administrative fees. These are entirely at the expense of the employer. They amount to a maximum of 5% of the AHV/IV/EO contribution, i.e. about 0.5% of the payroll total. If one's contributions exceed this amount, one can benefit from reduced administration costs if one submits the correct accounting documents and pay the contributions on time.

The AHV compensation fund collects the contributions for AHV/IV/EO, unemployment insurance and family compensation funds. In addition, premiums exist for obligatory accident insurance. These are invoiced by the accident insurer (for example, Suva for industrial companies) and are based on hazard classes and levels. Annual wages of up to CHF 148,200 are insured and subject to premiums. The employer bears the costs for work-related accidents and illnesses. The premiums for non-work-related accident insurance (NBUV) are partly or fully paid by employees.

The regulations regarding contributions to the pension fund are specific to each pension fund. It is stipulated by law that the employer must bear at least half of the costs of the entire pension contribution. Since the contribution rates for old-age savings increase with increasing age (at least the obligatory part), individual parity is not always guaranteed if a uniform contribution rate is levied for all employees at the same time.

9.3 Contributions to the state pension scheme by non-employed individuals

All Swiss residents who are not employed have AHV/IV/EO insurance and generally have to pay corresponding contributions.

Definition of non-employed individuals

Individuals who earn little or no income in Switzerland are considered inactive. This mainly includes the following groups of persons:

- Students
- World travelers
- Out-of-payment unemployed
- Wives and husbands of retired individuals
- Wives and husbands of spouses working abroad
- Retired individuals before reaching the standard AHV retirement age

Duration of contributions

After reaching the age of 20, the non-employed must pay contribution payments on 1 January. When AHV retirement age is reached, i.e. at the end of the month in which men reach the age of 65 and women reach the age of 64, no more payments are necessary.

Wives or husbands who are not employed but who reside in Switzerland are insured free of charge if the other spouse is insured and employed in the AHV/IV scheme and has paid the student contribution at least twice (CHF 976 per calendar year). This applies to the whole calendar year of the marriage term. However, non-employed individuals must pay contributions throughout the whole year in which their spouse dies or in which their divorce becomes legal.

If the working spouse is employed abroad for a certain period of time, and the family also resides abroad, the employer in Switzerland must ensure that the employee continues to be insured under the AHV/IV scheme. In this case, the accompanying non-working wife or husband must declare in writing that he/she is a member of the AHV/IV. This must be done through the relevant AHV compensation fund. Only then is the non-working person still insured, free of charge. This also applies to legal partnerships.

Calculation of contributions

Basis of calculation for taxpayers

Non-working individuals must pay contributions based on their assets and any capitalized replacement income (pension income, daily allowances etc.).

All domestic and foreign assets (including the spouse's and children's assets) and the value of life insurance policies are decisive in each case. The assets are valued on 31 December of the contribution year.

Replacement income (gross income) includes the following:

- Daily allowances for accident and health insurance (regardless of whether they are part of social or private insurance)
- Pensions of all kinds (excluding only disability pensions from the first pillar), but including international pensions
- Children's pensions to which the children have no entitlement of their own; these include, for example, children's disability insurance (BVG)
- Insurance or welfare benefits in Switzerland and abroad (such as benefits from pension funds, welfare foundations, group or individual insurances, etc.)

- Alimony and life annuities in Switzerland and abroad (for example, from a divorce settlement, but does not include children's alimony)
- Regular contributions from third parties, scholarships and similar grants
- Earned income of the husband or wife who is not subject to Swiss social security contributions

However, income from assets (interest on securities, rent and rental income, etc.) and capital gains are not defined as replacement income.

Basis of calculation for flat-rate taxpayers

For those subject to flat-rate tax, the agreed cost of living or the five-fold rental value is calculated as a pension income. It is multiplied by 20 in order to obtain the tax base. For married couples, half of the cost of living, multiplied by 20 is used as the basis for the calculation.

The AHV compensation fund in cantons where taxpayers pay wealth tax at a flat rate, uses the assets agreed in the context of flat-rate taxation instead of actual assets. For married couples, half of the agreed assets are used as a basis for the calculation.

In cantons where taxpayers pay wealth tax at a flat rate, the maximum contribution is usually CHF 23,900 per person per year. This is justified by the fact that the maximum contribution to be paid is for assets of CHF 8.4 million or more, and that the assets of most flat-rate taxpayers are of greater value than this amount. In addition, by paying the maximum amount, the assets do not have to be disclosed, which is convenient for many flat-rate taxpayers.

Calculating contributions

The minimum contribution to AHV/IV/EO is CHF 478 per person per year. This amount is adjusted periodically (usually every two years) to take inflation into account. Since 2012, the maximum contribution has been 50 times the minimum contribution, i.e. CHF 23,900 per person per year. The AHV compensation funds levy additional administrative fees of up to 5% of the total contribution.

The minimum contribution is owed by those with assets of less than CHF 300,000, by students up to the age of 25 (if older, their actual assets are assessed), and by individuals with supplementary benefits in addition to AHV/IV or social security benefits.

Table 9.4 Contribution table for non-working individuals from 2016 onwards

ASSETS WITH 20 TIMES THE ANNUAL PENSION INCOME (CHF)		AHV/IV/EO-CONTRIBUTIONS PER CALENDAR YEAR (CHF)
– under	300,000	478.00
– from	300,000	512.50
– from	350,000	615.00
– from	400,000	717.50
– from	450,000	820.00
– from	500,000	922.50
– from	550,000	1,025.00
– from	600,000	1,127.50
– from	650,000	1,230.00
– from	700,000	1,332.50
– from	750,000	1,435.00
– from	800,000	1,537.50
– from	850,000	1,640.00
– from	900,000	1,742.50
– from	950,000	1,845.00
– from	1,000,000	1,947.50
– from	1,050,000	2,050.00
– from	1,100,000	2,152.50
– from	1,150,000	2,255.00
– from	1,200,000	2,357.50
– from	1,250,000	2,460.00
– from	1,300,000	2,562.50
– from	1,350,000	2,665.00
– from	1,400,000	2,767.50
– from	1,450,000	2,870.00
– from	1,500,000	2,972.50
– from	1,550,000	3,075.00
– from	1,600,000	3,177.50
– from	1,650,000	3,280.00
– from	1,700,000	3,382.50
– from	1,750,000	3,485.00
– from	1,800,000	3,638.75
– For each additional CHF 50,000 the contribution increases by CHF 153.75 per year.		
The maximum contribution of CHF 23,900 per year is charged for assets of CHF 8.4 million and above.		

Source: AHV/IV Information office, 'Contributions of inactive persons to AHV, IV and EO', Leaflet 2.03 pp 5–6 (1 January 2018).

Pension

Contributions for individuals who are not fully employed throughout the year

In determining a person's contribution status as employed or non-employed, the AHV looks at the full calendar year. It also works to define the status of individuals who are not continually in full-time employment throughout the year (for example, part-time employees, persons in early retirement, persons who have been ill for a prolonged period, or who have been involved in an accident) and sets a value cap. For a person to be considered employed throughout a particular calendar year, at least half of their contribution must be covered by employment contributions (employer and employee contributions combined). Otherwise, the full non-employed contribution is due. Contributions paid from employment can be offset on request.

Procedure

Non-employed individuals who are not already covered by compulsory contributions, are obliged to register with the cantonal AHV compensation fund at their place of residence or the AHV municipal branch. Initially contributions are calculated by means of a self-declaration (detailed questionnaire), and then on the basis of the tax return.

The local cantonal AHV compensation fund of the non-employed person is responsible for this procedure. For students, it is the cantonal fund at the place of study. Those who take early retirement from the age of 58 continue to belong to the AHV compensation fund where they were last employed.[3] If necessary, the non-employed spouse is also recorded there (married couples must always be registered with the same AHV compensation fund).

Those who are not employed often forget to register with their relevant compensation fund when they take up residence, because they are not usually informed about their obligation to pay contributions. This leads to late payment of contributions and correspondingly high interest on arrears. Those moving to Switzerland must take responsibility for contribution payments themselves, and should contact their local AHV compensation fund or the AHV branch office within the first few weeks after taking up residence and fill out the questionnaire for inactive persons.

The AHV compensation funds calculate those contributions that are usually payable on a quarterly basis. These are provisional contributions, based on the person's prospective pension income and assets as no tax assessment will have been made at that point. It is therefore important to provide the compensation fund with

3 art 64 AHVG

copies of pension income statements to ensure that the assessment is as accurate as possible. As soon as the value of pension income or assets changes significantly, the compensation fund must be informed.

Final contributions are calculated by comparing the assessments of the cantonal tax authorities. The compensation funds calculate the difference between the paid contributions and the final contributions, refunding any overpaid contributions and invoicing for any further amounts due. This is to be paid within 30 days.

- Every person who pays social security contributions or receives corresponding benefits in Switzerland receives a 13-digit social security number. This can be found on the back of one's Swiss health insurance card. One can register at one's local AHV branch in order to obtain an insurance certificate
- The insurance certificate is the size of a credit card and must be carefully kept as it is an important document. The number of the insured person is repeatedly requested when dealing with social security funds and authorities

9.4 Benefits of state provision

The benefits of AHV

Old-age and survivors' insurance provides the following benefits:

- Survivors' pensions
- Old-age pensions, possibly with children's pensions
- Helplessness allowance for persons of retirement age
- Aid for people of retirement age

Entitlement to an old-age pension arises upon reaching the standard retirement age; 65 years for men, and 64 years for women. It is possible to make an advance withdrawal 12 or 24 months in advance, but this results in a reduction of the pension amount (reduction of 6.8% per year of prepayment). The withdrawal of the AHV pension can also be deferred by 12 to 60 months, with a corresponding surcharge (ranging from 5.2% to 31.5%). Advanced withdrawal or deferral of pension payouts is not linked to employment. Parents with children under 18 years of age, or those in the education system up to the age of 25, receive a children's pension in addition to their old-age pension.

- It is important to submit one's pension application (official form, *ahv-iv.ch, Merkblätter & Formulare*) at least six months before the desired start date. The pension is not paid automatically because the AHV compensation funds are missing relevant information
- A postponement of the pension payout must be claimed at the normal retirement age with the relevant completed application form. Otherwise, the surcharge will not be paid out

Entitlement to a survivor's pension is granted from the month following the death of a family member as follows:

- Men whose wives have died leaving at least one child under the age of 18. The entitlement to a widower's pension expires once the child reaches 18. The child can continue to receive their pension for as long as he or she is still in the education system, up to 25 years of age
- Women whose husbands have died when either at least one child has survived the father (the age of the child does not matter), or the spouse is at least 45 years of age, and has been married for at least five years at the time of widowhood (years are not necessarily counted from the same marriage). Entitlement to the widow's pension ends with remarriage, death or when AHV (old-age pension) comes into force
- Children whose parents (father or mother) have died with an AHV insurance scheme in place receive an orphan's pension up to the age of 18. If they are still in the education system, the orphan's pension will be paid up to the age of 25

The pension amount is based on two main factors:

1. The contribution period, i.e. the ratio of the contribution years possible from the year of birth, to those contribution years actually completed with the AHV (if the number of contribution years are the same, one receives full pension, otherwise a 1/44 pension reduction per missing contribution year applies)
2. The average annual income, (educational and childcare credits are also taken into account)

It is useful to find out the value of one's pension in advance, since it usually corresponds to that of a whole IV pension, allowing one to ascertain (together with the pension fund's insurance certificate) what pension income is available in the event of disability; the remainder of living costs must then be covered by the personal provision (i.e. the third pillar). To calculate the value of one's AHV pension in advance, visit the AHV website or submit an application form (*ahv-iv.ch, Merkblätter & Formulare*).

The minimum value of a full pension (for example, for married couples without any contribution, before splitting) is CHF 1,175 per month whilst the maximum value of a pension is CHF 2,350 per month. For married couples, where both spouses receive an AHV pension, entitlements are reduced pro rata to 150% of the applicable full pension. For example, married couples can receive up to CHF 3,525 per month (since 2012).

The benefits of IV

Disability insurance aims to:[4]

a. Prevent, reduce or remedy disability by means of suitable, simple, and relevant measures
b. Cover any financial needs due to the disability within the set IV framework
c. Contribute to an independent lifestyle

There are three service areas where treatment does not fall under the responsibility of disability insurance (IV), but instead under health, accident, or military insurance. These service areas are discussed below.

1. Rehabilitation measures

- Medical treatment (only for minors, i.e. mainly treatment of birth defects)
- Integration measures to prepare for professional integration (social vocational rehabilitation with stress and development training, employment measures with business-related support at the workplace); mainly for people with mental disabilities
- Vocational measures such as vocational counseling, initial vocational training for young people with disabilities, retraining, job placement, in some cases capital support for starting self-employment

4 art 1 IVG

- Mobility aids, including disability-friendly conversion of the workplace
- Provided that the integration results in a loss of earning capacity, a daily allowance amounting to 80% of the last insured earnings, up to a maximum of CHF 326, plus CHF 9 per child

In social security law and especially in the IV it is important to distinguish between incapacity to work and occupational disability.

- **Incapacity to work**[5]
  Is the total or partial inability to perform reasonable work in the previous occupation or area of responsibility due to a physical or mental impairment. It calls for curative treatment or care (which is not the responsibility of IV), early intervention, mobility aids, integration measures, and associated daily allowances
- **Occupational disability; earning incapacity**[6]
  Is the total or partial loss of earning potential in the labor market, caused by a physical or mental impairment that still remains after reasonable treatment and integration. It calls for a pension and possibly for helplessness allowances

2. Pensions

Insured individuals who are 18 years or older are entitled to a pension if they:

- Cannot restore, maintain, or improve their earning capacity — their employability — or their ability to work in their area of responsibility through reasonable integration measures
- Have been incapacitated for at least 40% on average during one year without significant interruption, and if:
  - After the end of this year are at least 40% disabled
  - They have made at least three years of contributions (a regular pension)

3. Helplessness allowance, with the possibility of assistance contribution

Residents in Switzerland who, in their daily lives, require considerable amounts of help from third parties and/or personal supervision, are entitled to a helplessness allowance.[7] The financial situation of the individual is irrelevant.

For a long time, IV was perceived as a pension insurance rather than an integration insurance. The earlier integration measures can be started, the greater the likelihood of returning to work:

5 art 6 ATSG
6 art 7 ATSG
7 art 9 ATSG

- Early detection: If someone is absent from the workplace for more than 30 days in a row, or within one year. Clarification of whether early intervention and/or actual integration measures are needed. If so, IV application and execution can take place
- Integration/pension registration: May be submitted directly if it is clear that early intervention or integration measures are required, or if there is an incapacity for work due to poor state of health

Benefits of the occupational pension plan

There are two scenarios with corresponding occupational health benefits:

1. Benefits *without* occurrence of the insured event

These benefits include the entire occupational pension plan, i.e. the obligatory and supplementary part, including vested benefits and purchases, each bearing interest. The relevant provisions are contained in a special law, the Federal Act on Vested Benefits in Occupational Retirement, Survivors' and Disability Pension Plans (FZG). The aim is to enable the person leaving the pension fund to take the benefits that he or she would need if he/she were to re-enter the pension fund on the same terms and conditions. The issues involved are as follows:

- Transfer of the vested benefit, also known as the termination benefit, to the new pension fund by changing jobs
- Transfer to a vested benefits account or policy during a period of inactivity (where applicable, cessation of employment before the occurrence of the insured event)
- Cash payment, because of:
  - Commencement of self-employment (corresponding registration by AHV compensation fund)
  - Permanent departure from Switzerland (please note: if one moves to an EU or EFTA country and is employed there one must pay the portion of the compulsory pension provision to a vested benefits account or a pension fund account) for up to five years before reaching the normal AHV retirement age (only then is it possible to withdraw the amount)
- Pension compensation in case of divorce
- Purchase of residential property with funds from occupational pension provision (advance withdrawal or pledge)

Pension

The signature of the spouse (registered partner) is mandatory for the payment of vested benefits. It is recommended to provide an officially certified signature in order to prevent fraudulent claims.

2. Benefits *upon* occurrence of the insured event

Actual insurance benefits are regulated by the Federal Law regarding Occupational Pension Plans (*Bundesgesetz über die berufliche Vorsorge* — BVG). Since most pension funds are aware of all possible additional benefits (non-obligatory benefits), the regulations of the relevant pension institution or fund should be consulted.

A prerequisite for a benefit (capital or pension) is that the person who applies for it must be insured in a pension fund (whether as an employed person, or as a pensioner).

The following summarizes the cover:

- Old-age benefits: Generally the AHV retirement age applies; however, the regulations may provide for retirement from the age of 58, gradual retirement with full continued insurance, or a continuation of insurance for individuals employed beyond retirement age
- Survivors' benefits: Widows and widowers are covered in the same way under mandatory insurance plans
- Widow's/widower's indemnity: Three times the lost annual pension as widow or widower if no survivor's pension is owed due to a lack of maintenance obligations towards children, lack of five years of marriage, or if the 45-year-old threshold has not been reached
- Disability benefits if the IV (first pillar) has confirmed a level of disability of at least 40% from the income comparison

9.5 Effects of the Agreement on the Free Movement of Persons between Switzerland and the European Community (EU)

The Agreement on the Free Movement of Persons (FZA) covers cross-border movement of persons in the narrower sense, coordination of social security, and mutual recognition of professional qualifications.

The coordination of the social security systems in the EU did not unify them. The 28 EU member states continue to structure their social security systems according to their own needs and economic situations.

Switzerland adopted the provisions of the FZA that govern the coordination of social security.[8] These provisions cover the following:

- Priority of the bilateral agreement over possible country agreements
- Subordination to the law of a state (simultaneously, only the national legislation of a member state is applicable)
- Equal treatment/non-discrimination (benefits in kind)
- Equal treatment of facts
- Total of insurance periods for all benefits
  - Pro-rata for pensions
- Export of services for cash benefits
- Benefits in kind
- Administrative assistance and cooperation of public authorities and institutions, electronic data correspondence

The same rules apply for other EFTA countries like Liechtenstein, Iceland, and Norway. That does not mean, however, that an Austrian working for a Swiss company in Norway is subject to the provisions of the FZA.

The provisions of the agreement apply to citizens of one of the EU states or Switzerland, who work in a member state that is not their own (for example, cross-border commuters), or who change residence from one member state to another. The starting point is employment that also applies to pensioners and persons receiving unemployment benefits. In the case of inferred claims (for example, children's pensions for disability, or survivors' pensions), non-employed individuals are also included. In the case of an application by a parent or spouse, the nationality of the non-employed spouse and of the children is irrelevant.

As social security legislation is subject to the law of only one state for employed individuals, clear rules have been established and are disclosed below:

Anyone who lives in one member state but works exclusively in another, is subject to the social security system in the country of work. However, if one is also employed in the member state where one is resident, one's income is subject to the laws of that state, providing that one spends 25% of one's time or earns 25% of one's income there. This may mean that a Swiss employer has to settle accounts with, for example, the French social security fund, because an employee from Alsace works from home (home office) one day a week and helps at the weekly market (in Alsace) on Saturdays.

8 reg 883/04 and implementing provisions 987/09, supplemented by 465/12

Those who work for only one employer and do not earn any significant amount of income in their country of residence (less than 25%), are subject to social security contributions at the employer's registered office. A self-employed individual in one member state who is also an employee in another, shall be subject to the system of that state where he/she is working. Self-employed or employed status is determined by the state, based on its particular legislation regarding that particular role. In Switzerland, for example, members of a board of directors are considered to be employed; the same applies to managing directors of a limited company, irrespective of the amount of equity invested.

Cash benefits can be taken abroad when necessary. For cash benefits (especially pensions), some states require a minimum contribution period (for example, Germany and Austria). Anyone who has been employed in Switzerland for a certain number of years and has paid contributions will not be left empty-handed. The Swiss Compensation Fund liaises with the EU and prepares the relevant documents for the pension insurance institution in the respective country. If the minimum contribution period is met, taking into account the insurance period completed in Switzerland (total sum of the insurance period), the individual is entitled to a pension that is proportional to the contribution period (pro-rata system). It may therefore be the case that a pensioner receives a partial pension from several countries on the basis of the provisions there.

This chapter provided an overview of the Swiss pension system and the country's social security funds and schemes. It also provided details of the obligatory contributions for employed and non-employed individuals residing in Switzerland.

Links to useful online resources

- *ahv-iv.ch*
  Homepage of the AHV compensation funds and IV offices, with information sheets and forms regarding AHV, disability insurance, income compensation for service providers, and in the case of maternity, family allowances, supplementary benefits for AHV/IV, and the receipt of contributions for unemployment insurance

- *arbeit.swiss.ch*
  Information sheets and forms for unemployment insurance, regarding unemployment compensation, short-time work, bad weather and insolvency compensation, as well as labor market measures
- *seco.admin.ch*
  Work, employment services, employment agencies, personnel hire, unemployment figures, short-time work, labor market analysis, job and family, women and career, older workers, protection of employees, etc.
- *bag.admin.ch*
  Federal Office of Public Health; information on health and accident insurance
- *bsv-admin.ch*
  Federal Social Insurance Office, offering information on social security funds
- *sfbvg.ch*
  Homepage of the BVG security fund, liaison for occupational benefits with specific background information on the cash payment of vested benefits, and forgotten pension fund assets
- *gebo.ch*
  Interaction of social security funds, current contribution rates and benefits, updates on social security funds

About the author

GERTRUD E. BOLLIER is a certified social insurance actuary and Managing Director of gebo Sozialversicherungen AG. She is active as a lecturer, consultant, and author of several publications in the field of comprehensive social security.

10 Health Insurance

Verena Nold, santésuisse, Solothurn

Anyone living in Switzerland can access the country's high-quality healthcare system via their compulsory basic health insurance (*Obligatorische Krankenpflegeversicherung or Grundversicherung*). In addition to this basic insurance, one can opt to extend one's cover to meet various personal needs with a voluntary supplementary insurance (for example, to cover costs for hospital stays or for alternative medicine treatment). Basic health insurance is offered by around 50 private health insurers, outlined in the Health Insurance Act (KVG). The individual insurers offer coverage for the same range of treatments, which are all recorded in the KVG catalog, and differentiate themselves by offering different product combinations and pricing structures.

Health insurance is based on four basic principles:

- Compulsory insurance: basic health insurance is obligatory for the entire population. However, all health insurers are obliged to include all individuals in their basic health insurance plans, regardless of the state of their health or their age
- Fairness: the structure of basic health insurance guarantees equal treatment for the healthy and the sick, young and old, men and women, and for everyone, regardless of their economic background
- Guaranteed access to treatments: in the event of illness, basic health insurance guarantees the insured individual access to all basic services
- Freedom of choice: insured individuals can choose their health insurance provider, their doctor, and their hospital — provided that the chosen insurance model does not have restrictions in place

10.1 Compulsory basic health insurance

Compulsory coverage

Health insurance is compulsory and must be proactively applied for.

All individuals must sign up with a health insurance provider within three months of taking up residence, or being born, in Switzerland. Minors must be insured by their legal guardians. Insurers are required to take on all applicants, provided that they reside within the insurer's area of activity. If the insurance fee is paid punctually, cover will apply retroactively from the start of residence or birth. If an individual signs up later than the required three months, no retroactive insurance cover is in place, and the individual is required to pay an additional premium.

With the Agreement on the Free Movement of Persons between the EU and the EFTA of 1 June 2002, all individuals from EFTA states working in Switzerland are required to take out compulsory basic health insurance. This also applies to any dependents who do not work. There are some exceptions for those residing in certain countries. For more detailed information on compulsory basic health insurance and the related options, go to *kvg.org*.

Each canton is responsible for compliance with the compulsory basic health insurance. Cantons inform their inhabitants about their insurance obligations and allocate a health insurance provider to anyone who does not apply for insurance within the given timeframe. It is also the prerogative of the canton to permit any exemptions from compulsory basic health insurance.

Treatments offered as part of compulsory basic health insurance

Compulsory basic health insurance plans also cover maternity needs and accidents. Accidents are, however, only covered if the insured individual has no other compulsory or private health insurance. The medical treatments covered by compulsory basic health insurance are comprehensive. Other than the insured person's agreed share of the costs (excess and deductible amounts), basic insurance covers all costs incurred by visiting a doctor's surgery, or hospital. Maternity care is fully insured covering pregnancy, childbirth, and post-natal care. Also included are, for example, laboratory examinations, prescription medicines, care at home, transport costs, and certain examinations. Dental treatments are not covered, with just a few exceptions.

All providers of compulsory basic health insurance are legally required to offer the same treatments and may not offer any additional treatments or benefits. For example, if a doctor recommends a treatment that is not included in the compulsory health insurance treatment catalog he/she is obliged to notify his/her patient.

Complementary medicine

Compulsory basic health insurance covers costs for acupuncture, anthroposophic medicine, homeopathy, phytotherapy, traditional Chinese medicine, and numerous other forms of complementary medicines. Other complementary medical treatments used for the detection, treatment, or prevention of diseases and disorders can be covered by private supplementary insurance.

Treatment abroad

Compulsory basic health insurance does not cover medical treatments abroad, except in emergency situations. If it is not possible for an individual to return to Switzerland for medical reasons, then the insurance plan will cover emergency treatment abroad for up to a maximum of twice the amount that the same treatment would have cost in Switzerland.

Premiums and choice of health insurance provider

In Switzerland each individual must be covered by the basic health insurance plan, including children and dependants. For example, a family of four will pay two adult premiums and two child premiums.

This system ensures that the healthy and the sick are treated equally. It also reflects the costs of the Swiss healthcare system. If the costs increase, the premiums increase. In contrast to an income-related system, all insured individuals are faced with the challenge of cost increases in health insurance, leading to increased awareness regarding this topic.

Insurance premiums are based on the age of the person, their place of residence, and their health insurance provider. Men and women pay the same premium. The law requires health insurance providers to accept any applicant regardless of their state of health or age. Everyone has the right to choose their health insurance provider.

Insured individuals are also free to change their compulsory basic insurance provider every six months, subject to a three-month notice period. If the insured individual has, however, selected an optional excess, or has taken out additional insurance, he/she may only change provider at the end of the year. If there is a change in the premium amount, the individual is able to switch health insurance provider at the end of the month preceding the introduction of the new premium. The difference in premiums between the various providers can be significant and it is worth comparing prices using the Federal Office of Public Health's premium calculator (*priminfo.ch*) or those of commercial providers (*comparis.ch* or *bonus.ch*). In this case, the notice period is one month. It is only possible to switch between compulsory basic health insurance providers if the individual has no payment defaults with the previous insurer, and has continuous insurance coverage, i.e. if the change to the new insurer is seamless. Compulsory basic health insurance ends only if the individual moves abroad, or upon the death of the individual.

Cost sharing

Invoices issued by GPs are usually sent to the patient to be paid directly. The patient then submits the invoice to the health insurer for reimbursement. Invoices for hospital treatments are usually submitted directly to the health insurance provider by the hospital for direct payment. In addition to the monthly premium, the individual contributes to the cost of any treatment received via the excess, and the patient contribution.

Excess

Each calendar year, insured individuals pay a certain percentage towards costs for doctors' fees, hospital visits, or prescriptions by contributing a fixed annual amount of CHF 300 (standard excess). This part of the cost sharing model is called the excess. Only when the cumulative costs exceed the agreed excess does the health insurance provider fully take over payments. The excess is paid once each calendar year and does not apply to children.

The legal excess amount is CHF 300 for adults and CHF 0 for children. However, this amount can be voluntarily increased by individuals in order to receive a premium rebate. An insurance plan with a higher excess is available to everyone but can only be agreed at the beginning of a calendar year. Switching to a lower excess is also possible within the set notice periods. Excess options of CHF 500; CHF 1,000; CHF 1,500; CHF 2,000; or CHF 2,500 are open to adults and young adults, whilst excess options of CHF 100; CHF 200; CHF 300; CHF 400; CHF 500; and CHF 600 are available for children (as of August 2017).

The costs to cover pre-natal check-ups, births, post-natal consultations, and lactation consultations are not included in the excess calculation.

Patient contribution

Patient contribution refers to the amount that the individual pays towards each treatment (doctor's fee, hospital stay, or prescriptions). Unlike the excess, this amount is not arbitrary.

If the cumulative costs exceed the agreed excess, the health insurance provider will cover the extra costs. However, the patient contribution forms 10% of these further excess costs, with a cumulative maximum cap of CHF 700 per calendar year (CHF 350 for children). The patient contribution for brand-name medicines, where a generic drug is also available, is 20%.

Patient contributions do not apply to pre-natal check-ups, births, post-natal consultations, or lactation consultations, nor do women have to contribute to their treatment for complications or illness from the 13th week of pregnancy, up to eight weeks after the birth. Complications in the first trimester of pregnancy are categorized as illness, and the patient contribution applies during this period.

Patients must pay a fee of CHF 15 per day for hospital stays regardless of patient contribution or excess option. This does not apply for maternity treatment, or for children and young adults in the education system who are between 18 and 25 years of age.

The patient contribution is the amount that the insured person has to bear for each benefit — doctor, hospital, or medication — himself/herself. Unlike the franchise, this amount is not eligible.

Alternative insurance models

Most health insurance providers offer a range of cheaper insurance options but by choosing one of these the individual must comply with certain requirements.

Health Maintenance Organization (HMO) model

There are a number of health centers, mainly located in urban areas, staffed by doctors full-time. An individual on the HMO model will be cared for at such a health centre if he/she falls ill. Even in emergencies, the HMO doctor is the first port of call. The price reduction for this option can be up to 20%.

GP model

The GP model is based on an association of doctors who have signed a contract with the health insurance provider. The individual selects his/her personal family doctor from a list and agrees to consult this doctor as a first step in the case of illness. Only when the illness requires treatment is the patient referred to a specialist. The price reduction for this option can be up to 20%.

Telephone consultation (Telmed model)

With the Telmed model, the individual agrees to seek telephonic advice before his/her first visit to the doctor. Based on the information given, medical specialists will make an initial assessment, offer recommendations, or refer the patient to a doctor or hospital. The price reduction for this option can be up to 15%.

There are also insurance models under which the individual agrees to use only those doctors or hospitals designated by the health insurance provider. Unlike with the GP model, the doctor can be chosen on a case-by-case basis.

Premium reductions

The basic health insurance system does not take into account the differences in the population's income. Therefore, the Swiss Confederation and the individual cantons grant premium subsidies to individuals in challenging economic circumstances. Insurance premiums for children and young adults in the education system are reduced by at least 50% if the parents have a small or medium income. The cantons determine the exact price reduction. The basis for distribution is the tax system, but significant price differences can arise. The subsidies are doled out in the form of discounts via the health insurance provider.

10.2 Optional supplementary insurance

While all aspects of compulsory basic health insurance must follow strict legal requirements, health insurance providers may create their own supplementary insurance packages, and set their own premiums. Insurers are also free to add restrictions to their supplementary insurance products, and even turn down an applicant, which is not permitted with compulsory basic health insurance.

In the case of supplementary insurance, it is important to differentiate between supplementary hospital insurance and the various, less costly supplementary outpatient insurance options, for example, cover for complementary medicine, dental treatment, psychotherapy, non-essential prescriptions, glasses, cover abroad, etc.

The following table shows the main differences between compulsory basic health insurance and supplementary insurance.

Table 10.1 Differences between compulsory basic health insurance and supplementary insurance

	COMPULSORY BASIC HEALTH INSURANCE	SUPPLEMENTARY INSURANCE
Basis of insurance	Legal and regulated.	Insurance contract includes general terms and conditions.
Acceptance by the insurance provider	Obligatory. The provider is legally required to accept all applicants.	No obligation to accept applicants.
Treatments	The treatment catalog is defined by law.	The insurer determines which supplementary benefits to offer in addition to the compulsory basic health insurance.
Setting of insurance premium	Standard premiums for each insurance provider and region. Premium reductions available. Lower premiums with higher excess/restriction on choice of service providers.	No restrictions. However, the competition is encouraging. Risk-adjusted premiums (often premium reductions available by choosing higher cost participation and with a no-performance discount).
Termination of insurance policy	The insurer cannot terminate the insurance policy. There is a one-month notice period on the part of the individual, at the end of every six months, whilst excess options can only be chosen at the end of the year. The policy cannot be terminated if there are outstanding payments owed.	Three-month notice period. Both parties can terminate immediately if an insurance claim is made (up to 14 days after payment). Most insurers withhold this right from their clients.
Exceptions when changing provider	Not permitted.	Unlimited; exclusion from certain treatments also possible.
Duration of coverage	Unlimited.	Policies can be for a fixed term (without renewal policies are automatically renewed for a year).
Treatment limitation	After five years.	After two years.
Possibility of joining a group insurance plan	No.	Yes.

Health Insurance

Cover

Outpatient supplementary insurance can cover complementary medicine treatments, non-compulsory prescriptions, glasses, contact lenses, and dental treatment. There is usually an annual cap on treatment costs.

There are two options for supplementary hospital insurance: the semi-private option or the private option. With the semi-private supplementary insurance option, the individual is entitled to a bed in a two-bed room in the case of a hospital stay. In public hospitals, the senior physician is usually responsible for the treatment of semi-privately insured patients. With the private supplementary insurance option, the individual is entitled to stay in a single room. In public hospitals, the head physician is usually responsible for the treatment of privately insured patients. Some insurers also offer flexible insurance models whereby it is only decided upon hospital admission whether the patient will stay in a general, semi-private, or private ward.

Premium

The premium is based on the treatments included in the policy, the individual's place of residence, his/her age, gender, and health insurance provider.

Cost sharing

With the supplementary hospital insurance offered by most insurers, the individual contributes to hospital treatments via the excess.

10.3 Accident cover

Those who move to Switzerland without employment are obliged to take out accident cover in addition to their compulsory basic insurance. The individual is entitled to treatment, meals, and accommodation in the general ward of the nearest hospital. If medical treatment is required abroad, the insurance plan will cover emergency treatment for up to a maximum of twice the amount that the same treatment would have cost in Switzerland.

Those who are employed by a single employer for at least eight hours per week are permitted to take out compulsory basic health insurance without accident cover as they are automatically insured by their employer against accidents, including accidents that occur out of office hours.

Anyone who wants to stay in a twin room (semi-private option) or in a single room (private option) during a hospital stay, or would like the option to choose the hospital or doctor, requires supplementary hospital insurance with accident cover.

If one does not want to forego additional outpatient treatments after an accident (for example, non-medical psychotherapy or natural healing sessions), one must also take out additional outpatient insurance with accident cover.

10.4 Residence registration

The process for compulsory basic health insurance

Individuals taking up residence in Switzerland must acquire basic health insurance and accident cover from a Swiss health insurance provider (for exceptions see s 10.6).

This compulsory basic health insurance does not have to be activated upon arrival to the country, or when registering residence. However, it is required that the compulsory basic health insurance is taken out within three months of residence registration, proof of which must then be submitted to the local municipality or the health department of the relevant canton. Most of the cantons provide a form for this process that is given to the individual upon residence registration.

By registering within the specified period of three months, retroactive insurance will apply from the start date of residence. The premiums also need to be paid retroactively too, and an entire month's premium is charged even for incomplete months.

If an individual signs up later than the required three months, no retroactive insurance cover applies and cover will only start from the date on which the health insurance was purchased. In this case the individual is also required to pay a late penalty premium. If no valid compulsory basic health insurance is acquired, the relevant local authority will automatically allocate an insurance provider to the individual.[1]

As the compulsory basic health insurance is compulsory, no health check is needed.

The process for supplementary insurance

Health insurance providers are permitted to ask questions about the health of the applicant applying for supplementary insurance. Based on a questionnaire and the health history of the applicant, the insurer may require additional health checks to be carried out by a medical practitioner. With this information, the health insurance provider may require certain temporary or permanent conditions from the applicant. This means that the individual is not covered for those treatments that are not specifically listed.

Most health insurers in Switzerland only accept new entrants for supplementary hospital insurance up to the age of 55. A few insurers accept applicants up to the

1 *Stadt Zürich, Städtische Gesundheitsdienste, 'Obligatorische Krankenversicherung'* Information sheet

age of 65. For older age groups, an international health insurance option may be worth considering (see section 10.5).

10.5 International health insurance providers

In some cases it is advisable to consider taking out health insurance with an international health insurance provider.

The main advantage of this option is that it offers one full international mobility. The individual can remain with the health insurance provider regardless of where he/she might reside in the future or how often he/she changes place of residence. The insurer has no right to cancel the policy when the individual moves abroad, unlike in the case of Swiss health insurers. As such, an international insurance policy is highly recommended for those who do not know in which country they will spend their retirement. If one takes out a policy with a Swiss health insurance provider and later moves to another country, one runs the risk of one's health worsening in the meantime, making it impossible to find additional insurance abroad.

Most health insurers in Switzerland only accept new entrants for supplementary hospital insurance up to the age of 55. A few insurers accept applicants up to the age of 65. In contrast, international health insurance providers offer options for older age groups, accepting applicants up to the age of 80, albeit for higher premiums.

One disadvantage of having international health insurance is that it often lacks recognition from the cantonal authorities. As such, exemption from Swiss compulsory basic health insurance is not always permitted (see section 10.6). In this case, the individual has to pay for both the Swiss compulsory basic health insurance, and the international health insurance premium, although this will mean that he/she had double cover for most treatments.

10.6 Exemptions from compulsory basic health insurance[2]

In certain cases, Swiss residents have no health insurance obligations, for example, if they are employed in, or receive a pension from an EU/EFTA state. Members of diplomatic or consular missions, as well as employees of international organizations with internationally recognized privileges are also not obliged to take out compulsory basic health insurance. EU/EFTA students strictly studying in Switzerland,

2 *Vgl. Gemeinsame Einrichtung KVG, Informationen für Aufenthalter (kvg.org -> Privatpersonen -> Versicherungspflicht -> Überblick)*

are also exempt from compulsory basic health insurance. Students from outside the EU/EFTA and privately insured students can be exempt if they have coverage that amounts to the equivalent of the Swiss basic health insurance.

Individuals may be exempt from compulsory basic health insurance in Switzerland, provided the following conditions[3] are met:

- The individual has compulsory health insurance in his/her home country and additional health insurance in Switzerland would be a double financial burden (this does not apply to persons from the EU/EFTA)
- The individual is following an education or training program in Switzerland (students, interns, trainees)
- A compulsory basic health insurance in Switzerland would offer a significantly poorer insurance policy than the previous private insurance cover, and due to the individual's state of health or advanced age, he/she would not be able to take out sufficient supplementary insurance in Switzerland. However, a significant increase in the insurance premium compared to the previous health insurance does not constitute a reason for exemption

Detailed information regarding compulsory basic health insurance and possible exemptions can be found on the KVG Foundation (*Gemeinsame Einrichtung KVG*) website. The KVG Foundation is an organization responsible for international treatment support, backed by parliament, the Federal Council, individual cantons, and the associations of health insurers.

Exemption owing to duplicate cover[4]

This regulation is rarely used, because in most countries regulations exist regarding social security, which is why there are only a few cases of people living and working in Switzerland who have statutory health insurance in their home country. This exemption is not applicable to individuals from the EU/EFTA or from a state with social security agreements that specify regulations on health insurance.

The following documents are required to support the application:

- Confirmation from the relevant foreign body regarding insurance cover for treatments in Switzerland (i.e. a similar insurance cover offered by the Swiss compulsory health insurance policies)

---

3 *Vgl. Gemeinsame Einrichtung KVG, Informationen für Aufenthalter (kvg.org -> Privatpersonen -> Versicherungspflicht -> Überblick)*

4 art 2 para 2 KVV

- Written confirmation that the individual has compulsory health insurance in his/her home country
- Copy of residence permit

Exemption owing to education/training programs[5]

Individuals taking part in compulsory education or training programs in Switzerland (i.e. students, pupils, interns and apprentices, and members of their families accompanying them), can request exemption from compulsory basic health insurance if they have equivalent coverage that is valid for their entire stay. The request must be accompanied by written confirmation from the responsible foreign body providing all the necessary information. The relevant cantonal authority is able to offer exemptions for three years. Upon request, the exemption may be extended for a maximum of a further three years. However, the individual must provide an excellent reason for the extension.

This rule applies to students from non-EU/EFTA states, as well as those who are privately insured.

The following documents are required to support the application:

- Confirmation from the relevant foreign body regarding insurance cover for treatments in Switzerland (i.e. a similar insurance cover offered by the Swiss compulsory health insurance policies)
- Confirmation of education/training program (for example, internship contract, matriculation certificate)

Expats[6]

The decisive factor in determining whether someone is an expat is the legislation the individual and his/her family members are subject to. In principle, an expat continues to be subject to the legislation of the country that he/she originates from. As soon as someone in Switzerland provides social security contributions such as pensions, life insurance, unemployment insurance, etc., the person is not considered an expat anymore.

The following documents are required to support the application:

- Confirmation from the relevant foreign body regarding insurance cover for treatments in Switzerland (i.e. a similar insurance cover offered by the Swiss compulsory health insurance policies)

5 art 2 para 4 KVV
6 art 2 para 5 KVV

- Written confirmation of expat status from the Office of Social Security or from the employer
- Copy of residence permit

EU/EFTA expats do not need to apply for exemptions. They are not required to take out compulsory basic health insurance in Switzerland.

Exemption for EU/EFTA citizens without employment[7]

In line with the Agreement on the Free Movement of Persons, those from EU/EFTA countries who have a residence permit for Switzerland but are without employment are exempt from the compulsory basic health insurance obligation, provided that they have equivalent insurance cover from a foreign insurer for treatment in Switzerland.[8]

The following documents are required to support the application:

- Confirmation from the relevant foreign body regarding insurance cover for treatments in Switzerland (i.e. insurance cover similar to that offered by the Swiss compulsory health insurance policies)
- Copy of residence permit

Health Insurance

This rule does not apply to unemployed individuals from EU/EFTA countries insured under a statutory health insurance system. They must be insured in Switzerland, their country of residence.

Exemption owing to poorer coverage than existing insurance cover[9]

A person can be exempt from compulsory basic health insurance in Switzerland if it offers a significantly poorer cover than the previously held private insurance cover, due to the individual's state of health or advanced age. However, an equivalent insurance policy does not constitute a reason for exemption. Coverage must go far beyond what is stipulated by the Federal Law on Health Insurance. In terms of age, an individual who is 55 years old or older may be eligible for an exemption. An individual's state of health, the diagnosis, and the related future treatments are taken into account when assessing whether additional insurance should be taken out in Switzerland or not. These exemptions are rarely offered.

---

7 art 2 para 7 KVV
8 art 2 para 7 KVV
9 art 2 para 8 KVV

The following documents are required to support the application:

- Written confirmation detailing the individual's health insurance (including treatment cover etc.)
- Medical certificate with diagnosis and necessary future treatments (if under 55 years of age)
- Proof of worsening conditions (regarding treatment and/or costs) compared to existing (previous) insurance cover
- As the Swiss insurance providers are not bound to prescribed tariffs for privately insured individuals, the foreign insurer must confirm that, in the case of an exemption, all costs for medical treatment in Switzerland will be assumed in full, without exception or limitation
- Copy of residence permit

Equivalent insurance cover

Equivalent insurance cover refers to the Swiss Federal Law on Health Insurance (KVG). The foreign insurance provider is obliged to pay the costs according to what the KVG would pay at the very least. For example, the foreign health insurance provider cannot impose caps (for example, cost per day, maximum insurance coverage, etc.), except when particularly high. In addition, all benefits paid in accordance with Swiss law must also be covered by the foreign insurance (such as maternity benefits, care while residing in Switzerland, etc.). The fact that compulsory health insurance in Switzerland usually does not cover the costs of dental treatment is not sufficient for an exemption.

International treatment assistance[10]

Individuals who receive a pension from and are insured in an EU /EFTA state, but who have residence in Switzerland, do not have to take out compulsory basic health insurance in Switzerland. Instead, they are subject to the relevant EU/EFTA state health insurance. Their non-working family members are not obliged to take out compulsory basic health insurance in Switzerland either.

Those who live in Switzerland, but are tied to the statutory health insurance system in their EU/EFTA countries, are entitled to so-called 'treatment assistance'. This scheme, which helps to cover costs for illnesses, non-occupational accidents, and maternity, is managed by the KVG Foundation.

10 *kvg.org* > *Privatpersonen* > Assistance

In order to receive medical treatment in Switzerland, an individual must obtain a certificate from his/her health insurance provider in the EU/EFTA country (for example, S1, E 106, E 121). This entitles him/her to reimbursement of the costs for basic health insurance benefits, in accordance with the Swiss Health Insurance Act (sickness, maternity, and accident benefits, provided that no accident insurance is liable for benefits). The entitlement and scope of benefits correspond to those of a person insured within the scope of the KVG in Switzerland, with the exception of daily allowances.

To receive basic treatment coverage, an individual and his/her family members must apply to the KVG Foundation, submitting the certificate issued by the foreign health insurance provider.

The costs for hospital treatment and stays are temporarily covered by the KVG Foundation. Subsequently, the foreign health insurance provider will be invoiced. For outpatient treatment, an individual usually has to pay the doctor's bill himself/herself (the tiers garant system) but can apply for a reimbursement from the KVG Foundation. The costs sharing specified by Swiss law is still applicable in this case.

In some cases, it is useful to take out a separate Swiss insurance to cover hospital stays and treatments.

Further information:
The KVG Foundation offers advice and information.
Address: Gemeinsame Einrichtung KVG, Gibelinstrasse 25, Postfach, CH-4503 Solothurn
Tel. +41 (0)32 625 30 30, Fax: +41 (0)32 625 30 29, *kvg.org*

This chapter provided an overview of the Swiss healthcare system. Switzerland has excellent compulsory basic health insurance and a variety of voluntary supplementary insurance options to suit the needs of individuals.

Useful online resources and addresses

- *bag.admin.ch*
  Federal Office for Public Health (FOPH) (*Bundesamt für Gesundheit* — BAG)
  The FOPH is dedicated to protecting public health and improving the country's healthcare system
  Address: *Bundesamt für Gesundheit*, CH-3003 Bern, Tel. +41 (0)31 322 21 11, Fax +41 (0)31 323 37 72
- *priminfo.ch*
  An official cost comparison website of the FOPH for all Swiss health insurance providers
- *kvg.org*
  Here one will find a number of application forms related to health insurance
- *gdk-cds.ch/index.php?id=724*
  The cantonal health authorities (*Die Gesundheitsdirektionen der Kantone*)
  The health authority of one's canton of residence can help with questions on health insurance coverage
- *secure.om-kv.ch*
  Health Insurance Ombudsman (*Ombudsstelle der sozialen Krankenversicherung*)
  The Ombudsman offers advice on disputes with Swiss health insurance providers.
  Address: Ombudsstelle der sozialen Krankenversicherung, Morgartenstrasse 9, CH-6003
  Lucerne, Tel. +41 (0)41 226 10 10, Fax +41 (0)41 226 10 13
- *santesuisse.ch*
  santésuisse
  santésuisse is the leading industry association of Swiss health insurance providers.
  Address: santésuisse, Römerstrasse 20, CH-4502 Solothurn,
  Tel. +41 (0)32 625 41 41

Health Insurance

About the author

VERENA NOLD is the Director of the Health Insurance Association santésuisse. From 2004 to 2010, she was vice-director of santésuisse, and responsible for negotiations regarding insurance premiums. Subsequently she was director of Tarifsuisse, a spin-off of santésuisse, responsible for negotations on premiums at national and cantonal level.

11 Matrimonial Property Law and Inheritance Law

Kinga M. Weiss, Walder Wyss

Matrimonial Property Law and Inheritance Law

Individuals who wish to take up residence in Switzerland should consider the potential implications of their relocation on the applicable rules in the area of matrimonial property law (or the respective rules for registered partners) and inheritance law. Pursuant to Swiss private international law, the main connecting factor in general is Swiss residence. If no precautions are taken prior to, or after moving to Switzerland, the change of residence might lead to unintended legal consequences for an individual's family affairs. Therefore, it is recommended to verify whether there is need to take any action prior to relocation.

Existing pre- or postnuptial agreements, as well as estate planning measures should be reviewed and, if necessary, adjusted to the new Swiss legal environment.

The following guidelines provide a brief overview of the various subjects in the area of matrimonial property law (or the respective rules for registered partners), and the law of inheritance, including the treatment of trusts in Switzerland. However, these guidelines are not meant to be complete or exhaustive.

11.1 Statutory provisions

Swiss matrimonial property law (the respective rules for registered partners) and inheritance law are essentially governed by the following Swiss statutes:

- Swiss Civil Code (CC)/*Schweizerisches Zivilgesetzbuch* (ZGB) of 10 December 1907[1]
  - art 181–251 CC: Swiss substantive law relating to matrimonial property law
  - art 457–640 CC: Swiss substantive law relating to inheritance law
- Federal Act on Registered Partnerships for Same-Sex Couples/*Bundesgesetz* über *die eingetragene Partnerschaft gleichgeschlechtlicher Paare* (PartG) of 18 June 2004[2]
- Practical modalities for the transfer (for example, affixing seals, drawing up the inventory, etc.), and allocation of succession are provided for in cantonal provisions
- Swiss Private International Law Act (SPILA)/*Bundesgesetz über das internationale Privatrecht* (IPRG) of 18 December 1987[3]

According to the SPILA,[4] the terms and conditions of international agreements take precedence over Swiss legislation. The most important conventions and treaties in the area of matrimonial property law, inheritance law, and trusts, which are applicable in Switzerland due to ratification, include:

- The Hague Convention of 1961 relating to the Form of Testamentary Dispositions
- The Hague Convention of 1985 relating to the Law Applicable to Trusts and on their Recognition

Switzerland has also concluded numerous bilateral conventions containing provisions on succession, such as:

- Treaty of 1850 concluded between the Swiss Confederation and the United States of North America (1855)[5]
- Treaty of 1855 of Friendship, Commerce and Reciprocal Establishment between the Swiss Confederation and Her Majesty the Queen of the United Kingdom of Great Britain and Ireland (1856)[6]
- Convention of 1868 of Establishment and Consular Relations between the Swiss Confederation and Italy (1869)[7]

1 SR 210
2 SR 211.231
3 SR 291
4 art 1 para 2 SPILA
5 art V and VI
6 art IV
7 art 17 (art IV of protocol of 1 May 1869)

11.2 Matrimonial property law

Swiss matrimonial property law deals with the effects of marriage on the spouse's rights to the marital assets in the event of divorce, or one spouse's death. In an international setting, as far as no treaty or bilateral convention is applicable, the relevant statute is the SPILA. The SPILA does not only determine which law systems and provisions should be applied (conflict of laws), but also determines the jurisdiction of Swiss courts and authorities in international matters, including recognition and enforcement of foreign judgments and decisions. Art 51 et seqq of the SPILA provides for the conflict of law rules regarding matrimonial property law.

Conflict of law rules

Spouses may designate the law they wish to apply to their matrimonial property regime.[8] They may choose the law of the state in which they are both domiciled, or where they will be domiciled after the marriage, or the law of a state in which either of them is a national.[9] The choice of law must be executed in writing.[10] The chosen law remains applicable as long as the spouses have not amended or revoked such a choice.[11]

In the absence of an agreement on choice of law, the division of property under the matrimonial property regime is carried out according to the law of the country where both spouses are domiciled, or were last domiciled at the same time.[12] If the spouses were never domiciled in the same state at the same time, their common national law applies. In case the spouses do not have a common nationality, the separation of property regime according to Swiss law applies.[13]

If the spouses transfer their domicile from one state to another the law of the new domicile applies and takes effect retroactively from the day of marriage.[14] However, the couple may exclude the retroaction, or agree to continue the application of the previous law by entering into a written agreement or a marital agreement.

Foreign marital agreement

In case the spouses have concluded a marital agreement under a foreign law prior to moving to Switzerland, the agreement will in general be recognized in Switzerland, meaning that the relocation to Switzerland does not automatically lead to the

8 art 52 para 1 SPILA
9 art 52 para 2 SPILA
10 art 53 para 1 SPILA
11 art 53 para 3 SPILA
12 art 54 para 1 SPILA
13 art 54 para 3 SPILA
14 art 55 para 1 SPILA

application of Swiss matrimonial property law. However, in the event the spouses live in Switzerland and they have not entered into a marital contract prior to moving to Switzerland, their matrimonial property rights will be subject to Swiss law unless (i) they both declare in writing that the former law shall remain applicable, or (ii) they issue a marital agreement for the application of the law of the state of their nationality. As far as the form of a foreign matrimonial property agreement is concerned, the agreement is regarded as valid from a Swiss legal perspective if it complies with the law governing the matrimonial property agreement, or with the law of the place of conclusion of the agreement.[15]

EU Regulations on matrimonial property regimes/property consequences of registered partnerships

To provide legal certainty for spouses/registered partners within an international setting, 18 EU member states passed the regulation on matrimonial property regimes,[16] and the regulation on property consequences of registered partnerships[17] on 28 July 2016. Together, these regulations form the EU Regulations on property law. Most of the provisions embedded in the regulations will come into force on 29 January 2019. Even though Switzerland is not a member of the EU, the regulations will still have an impact on spouses/registered partners living in Switzerland who are connected to one of the member states by their nationality, their habitual residence, or their assets.

In general, the EU Regulations on the property law regulate the applicable law (conflict of laws), determine which court and authorities may claim jurisdiction in international matters, and define the conditions for recognition and enforcement of foreign judgments and decisions. If a couple lives in Switzerland and one of the spouses/partners moves to a country in which the EU Regulations on property law apply, it may lead to a conflict of jurisdiction and applicable law, for example, if a divorce or succession proceeding is initiated, since Switzerland and the country of influx may both claim jurisdiction and apply their own laws. In order to avoid such conflicts it is important that spouses/partners living in Switzerland consider jointly agreeing on the jurisdiction and the law that shall be applicable to the matrimonial property/ the property for registered partners, to avoid any unintended legal consequences. Under the EU Regulations on property law, spouses and partners may choose the law of the state where the spouses/partners, or one of them, is habitually resident at the time the agreement is concluded, or the law of a state of nationality of either

15 art 56 SPILA
16 EU Regulation 2016/1103
17 EU Regulation 2016/1104

spouse/partner.[18] Registered partners may additionally choose the law of the state under which law the registered partnership was created.[19] The available legislative options according to Swiss international law are set out in section 11.1 above. It is in most cases recommended that spouses/partners try to align the substantive law that will govern the matrimonial property/property of the registered partnership, and the substantive law that will govern the estate of a deceased spouse, as these areas of law are usually closely linked in case a spouse/registered partner passes away. Furthermore, special attention has to be paid to the formal requirements of matrimonial property agreements/partnership property agreements. Different requirements exist for the formal validity of agreements depending on the partners' habitual residence, or the law chosen by the spouses/partners.[20] Hence, spouses/partners with international backgrounds cannot under the EU Regulations on property law rely solely on a matrimonial property agreement/partnership property agreement that satisfies the formal requirements of the state where it was signed, for example, in Switzerland, to be sufficient for the agreement to be formally valid.

Swiss substantive law

A consequence of the dissolution of a marriage by divorce, judicial separation, nullity or death, is that the marital assets must be divided between the spouses. The matrimonial property law regimes have an impact on the calculation of each spouse's share in the other spouse's assets in case of liquidation of the matrimonial property. In case of death, depending on the regime in place, a spouse is entitled to a specified share of the deceased's assets prior to the partition of the estate among the heirs.

Swiss law provides for three different matrimonial property law regimes from which the spouses may choose, namely:

(1) the ordinary matrimonial property regime of participation in acquired property
(2) the community of property
(3) separation of property

Ordinary regime of participation in acquired property[21]

This matrimonial property regime applies if the spouses have not chosen any extraordinary matrimonial property regime by marital agreement. Under this regime, each spouse retains and manages his/her own assets and acquisitions during

18 art 22 para 1 lit a and b of the EU Regulations on property law
19 art 22 para 1 lit c of the EU Regulation on property consequences of registered partnerships
20 art 25 of the EU Regulations on property law
21 art 196 ff CC

the marriage. A distinction is made between a spouse's own property (*Eigengut*) and the acquired property during marriage (*Errungenschaft*). A spouse's own property comprises the assets that were brought into the marriage, or were received through gifts or inheritance during the marriage. Acquired property includes in particular assets that resulted through employment or self-employment, or income derived from their own property during the marriage. By way of marital agreement, certain changes in this classification are possible.[22] Hence, each asset of the spouses is allocated either to acquired or owned property.

A spouse's own property is not subject to the division of property during the liquidation of the matrimonial property. Furthermore, spouses must settle what they owe each other, and the debts that they owe to third parties. A debt is charged to the property to which it is objectively connected or, in case of doubt, to the property acquired during marriage.[23] During the division of property, a compensation claim exists when acquisition debts were paid from the property of one spouse, or own property debts from the acquisitions of one spouse.[24] Increases or decreases in value must be calculated and assigned. If a spouse has contributed to the acquisition, improvement or preservations of assets of the other spouse, without compensation, and if an added value exists at the time of division, then the contributing spouse shall have a claim proportional to his/her contribution.[25]

The first step in the liquidation process is that each spouse (or the successors of the deceased spouse) takes back his/her assets that are in the other's possession,[26] and retains one-half of the property acquired by the other spouse during the marriage. By way of marital agreement, the spouses may deviate from certain aspects of this general rule.[27]

Community of property regime

Under the regime of community of property, which is subject to contractual modifications by the spouses, each spouse holds his or her personal property (for example, clothes, jewelry), while the other assets of the marriage are jointly owned and managed.[28] If the community of property regime is dissolved by death of a spouse, each party is entitled to an equal share in the common property.[29] On dissolution

22 art 199 CC
23 art 209 para 2 CC
24 art 209 para 1 CC
25 art 206 CC
26 art 205 para 1 CC
27 art 215 CC
28 art 222 CC
29 art 241 CC

of the marriage by divorce, the common property is divided, broadly following the rules governing the division under the acquired property regime. Irrespective of the marital agreement, each spouse takes back from the common property what, under the acquired property regime, would be his or her own property.[30] The remaining property held in common is divided in half, or according to the rules set out in the marital agreement. Spouses either need to act jointly, or with the consent of the other spouse to validly dispose of common property.[31]

Separation of property

If spouses have validly agreed to the matrimonial property regime of separation of property, pursuant to art 247 et seqq CC, a division of property is not necessary as there is no acquisition or common property that must be divided in case of divorce or death of one of the spouses. Each spouse retains his/her assets.

Civil partnership/same sex marriage

Since 1 January 2007, it is possible for persons of legal age to register their same-sex partnerships, and thereby legally secure their relationships, under the Swiss Federal Act on Registered Partnerships for Same-Sex Couples of 18 June 2004. In doing so, same-sex couples enjoy legal status equal to married couples, in the area of inheritance, social security, occupational pension plans, insurance, taxes, and immigration. Medical reproduction procedures for same-sex couples are forbidden. Same-sex couples may not adopt children together, but the adoption of stepchildren is possible for same-sex couples (since January 2018) if the general conditions for adoption are fulfilled. By law, the rules of the regime of separation of property apply with regard to their assets. However, the partners may enter into an agreement to have the provisions of the ordinary regime of acquired property apply.

11.3 Inheritance law

Inheritance law is intended to protect statutory heirs, which include children, the spouse, and if there are no children, the parents of the deceased. Basically, the law defines how the estate of a deceased has to be split between heirs. In an international setting, where no treaty or bilateral convention is currently applicable, the relevant statute is again the SPILA.

30 art 242 CC
31 art 228 CC

Conflict of law rules

Successions are covered in art 86 et seqq of the SPILA. It specifies the rules applicable to determine the jurisdiction to deal with succession, the law applicable to govern succession, and how decisions, measures and documents relating to succession, as well as rights pertaining to a succession probated abroad, are recognized in Switzerland when they have been made, taken or drawn up abroad.

As a general rule, the Swiss courts authorities have jurisdiction over probate matters and inheritance disputes in relation to the worldwide estate at the deceased's last domicile, with the exception of real estate where a foreign state claims exclusive jurisdiction.[32] The Swiss authorities (*Heimatort*) have jurisdiction at the deceased's place of origin when a Swiss national who died with his/her last domicile abroad, by will or inheritance contract, subjected his/her assets or entire estate in Switzerland to the jurisdiction of the Swiss courts, or to Swiss law.[33] Furthermore, the Swiss authorities are tasked to deal with the estate of a Swiss citizen at the place of origin of the deceased who died with his/her last domicile abroad if the foreign authorities do not deal with this estate.[34] Similarly, whenever a deceased with foreign nationality was last domiciled abroad and leaves assets in Switzerland, the Swiss authorities at the location of the assets have jurisdiction, and will open the succession procedure if the foreign authorities do not deal with the Swiss assets.[35]

The SPILA determines the law applicable to the succession where the Swiss courts or authorities have jurisdiction. When a person dies with his/her last domicile in Switzerland, his/her worldwide estate is governed by Swiss inheritance law.[36] When a person dies with his/her last domicile abroad, and the Swiss courts or authorities have jurisdiction, the estate is governed by the law as determined by the conflict of law rules of the foreign state.[37] Where the Swiss authorities are tasked to deal with the estate of a Swiss national with last domicile abroad, the estate is governed by Swiss law, unless the deceased has expressly made a choice of law in favor of the law of his/her last domicile by will or inheritance contract.[38] A foreigner with his/her domicile in Switzerland may subject his/her whole estate to the law of the country of his/her nationality.[39] Swiss citizens with dual nationalities are deemed to be Swiss citizens only and may thus not subject their estate to the law of the country of their other nationality.

32 art 86 SPILA
33 art 87 para 2 SPILA
34 art 87 para 1 SPILA
35 art 88 SPILA
36 art 90 para 1 SPILA
37 art 91 para 1 SPILA
38 art 91 para 2 SPILA
39 art 90 para 2 SPILA

Swiss law recognizes the concept of inheritance contracts, whereby two or several parties may regulate their succession with binding effect. Inheritance contracts are governed by the law of the domicile of the deceased at the time of the execution of the contract.[40] The deceased may, however, subject his/her entire estate to the law of his nationality.[41]

Recognition of foreign wills or inheritance contracts

The Swiss courts and authorities accept any foreign will or inheritance contract that complies with the requirements of the applicable law under the Hague Convention of 5 October 1961 regarding the form of testamentary dispositions.

EU Succession Regulation

In the same spirit as the EU Regulations on matrimonial property law/property consequences for registered partnerships, the EU Succession Regulation[42] (EU SR) aims to simplify estate planning and the administration of estates in an international setting by harmonizing the jurisdiction and applicable laws of international succession. The EU SR is applicable in 25 EU member states since 17 August 2015. Switzerland is not a member of the EU and is not adopting the rules stated in the EU SR. Nevertheless, it is important to consider the EU SR if persons domiciled in Switzerland have a connection to the EU, for example, if they own movable or immovable assets located in a member state.

In general, the EU SR assigns jurisdiction to the member state in which the deceased had his/her last habitual residence.[43] If the last habitual residence of the deceased at the time of death is not located in a member state, but in a third-country state such as Switzerland, the courts of the member state in which assets of the estate are located shall nevertheless have jurisdiction to rule on the succession as a whole in so far as (a) the deceased had the nationality of that member state at the time of death; or, failing that (b) the deceased had his/her previous habitual residence in that member state, provided that, at the time the court is seized, a period of not more than five years has elapsed since the location of his/her habitual residence has changed.[44] Where no court has jurisdiction pursuant to (a) or (b), then the courts of the state where the assets are located shall have jurisdiction to rule on those assets.[45]

40 art 95 para 1 SPILA
41 art 95 para 2 SPILA
42 EU Regulation 650/2012, EU SR
43 art 4 EU SR
44 art 10 (1) EU SR
45 art 10 (2) EU SR

The EU SR states that, generally, the law of the state in which the deceased had his/her last habitual residence, shall govern the estate.[46] A testator may choose a law provision in favor of the law of his/her nationality at the time of the choice of law, or the law of his/her nationality at the time of death,[47] to govern his/her worldwide estate. Hence, individuals residing in Switzerland owning assets in a member state, should consider the possible implications of the EU SR to avoid any unexpected results.

Swiss substantive law

General

Upon a person's demise, the estate passes directly to the heirs (either under the will or the intestacy rules), who automatically become joint owners of the entire estate (universal succession).[48] Therefore, all rights and liabilities of the deceased at the time of his/her death pass to the heirs. If the deceased leaves more than one heir, the heirs form a community of heirs, and are jointly entitled to all rights and liabilities of the estate until the estate is divided. The heirs are the owners and jointly dispose of the estate. If an executor has been appointed then he/she administers the estate for the heirs.

An heir can renounce his/her share in the estate within three months of becoming aware of the inheritance or in advance, for example, during the lifetime of the deceased, for or without consideration by an inheritance contract.

The testator may allocate an object or the usufruct of it, or compel heirs or legatees to pay someone from the inheritance, or to free someone from a duty. The testator may also oblige an heir to forward the inheritance to a third party, the reversionary heir, normally in the case of the former's death.

Intestacy

In the absence of a testamentary disposition, the statutory heirs inherit the entire estate. The shares of the statutory heirs depend on the relatives of the deceased being still alive at the time of the testator's death:

- Descendants with no surviving spouses: The deceased's descendants inherit the estate in equal shares
- Surviving parents with no descendants: The deceased's parents inherit the estate in equal shares. If one of the deceased's parents is deceased, that parent's descendants inherit that share. If the deceased parent does not have any other descendants, the entire estate passes to the surviving parent

46 art 21 EU SR
47 art 22 para 1 EU SR
48 art 457 to 640 CC

- Surviving grandparents with no surviving parents, brothers and sisters or nieces and nephews: The estate passes to the grandparents, or their descendants, in equal parts
- No surviving spouse, descendants, parents, siblings, or grandparents or their descendants: In the absence of any heir, the estate passes to the canton of the deceased's last domicile, or to the commune designated by the legislation of that canton

The spouse's share amounts to the following portions of the estate:
- $\frac{1}{2}$ if there are descendants
- $\frac{3}{4}$ if there are no descendants, but surviving parents or their descendants
- $\frac{1}{1}$ if there are no descendants, surviving parents, or their descendants

Pursuant to the Federal Law on Registered Partnerships of Same-Sex Couples, same-sex couples can have their partnership registered with the competent cantonal authority. With such registration, the surviving partner has the same statutory share of inheritance as a spouse, and is also entitled to a compulsory portion.[49]

Forced heirship rules

Swiss law contains forced heirship rules. A testator can freely dispose of his/her estate, but there are statutory limitations protecting certain categories of legal heirs who have a right to a compulsory portion of the estate (forced heirship right). It is the spouse and the descendants (and parents, if there are no descendants), who are protected under the forced heirship rules and they may file a claim of abatement if the testator violates their compulsory portion. As such, a testator may only dispose of the freely disposable portion of his/her estate through testamentary dispositions.

The compulsory portion amounts to a specified fraction of the statutory share:
- For the spouse: $\frac{1}{2}$ of his/her statutory share
- For the descendants: $\frac{3}{4}$ of their statutory share
- For the parents: $\frac{1}{2}$ of their statutory share

These rules result in the following freely disposable portions:
- If there is a spouse, but no descendants or surviving parents, the freely disposable portion is $\frac{1}{2}$
- If there is a spouse and descendants, the freely disposable portion is $\frac{3}{8}$

49 art 471 para 3 CC

- If there is a spouse and parents, the freely disposable portion is $\frac{1}{2}$
- If there is no spouse, but descendants, the freely disposable portion is $\frac{1}{4}$
- If only parents survive, the freely disposable portion is $\frac{1}{2}$

The compulsory portion is calculated as follows, by considering certain *inter vivos* gifts made by the deceased, in particular:

- The net value of all the assets held by the deceased at the time of his/her death
- Inheritance advances
- Lifetime gifts made by the deceased within five years prior to his/her death
- Lifetime gifts (no time limit) that have the evident purpose of evading the forced heirship rules

An heir entitled to a compulsory share has the right to receive the full amount of such a share outright and the testator may not impose a charge on the compulsory portion, for example, by means of a trust or by attaching conditions.

A testator's disposition may provide grounds for an action of abatement[50] if it violates forced heirship rights. Such claim has to be fixed within one year of having noticed the violation.[51]

Wills and inheritance contracts

There are three forms of wills recognized under Swiss law: (i) holographic wills, (ii) notarized public wills, and (iii) oral wills (in cases of emergency, where the testator is no longer in a position to make a will). The holographic will is the most common form of will.[52] It must be written in the testator's own handwriting from start to finish, including an indication of the date and the signature of the testator. Swiss law also provides for inheritance contracts by which the testator leaves the inheritance, or a bequest, to a third person or to his/her contracting party. A testator's heir may also enter into an inheritance contract with the testator, to renounce in advance all or part of his/her rights of inheritance in the estate, with or without consideration.

A testator may either revoke a will by destroying the deed,[53] or by declaring it invalid, using one of the forms required for the drawing up of a will,[54] or by making a subsequent will. Where a testator makes a new will without expressly revoking

50 art 522 para 1 CC
51 art 533 para 1 CC
52 art 505 CC
53 art 510 CC
54 art 509 CC

an earlier one, it is presumed by law that the latest shall supersede the preceding one, unless the latest will clearly purports to be a supplementary disposition only.[55]

An inheritance contract is considered as valid if the formalities required by a public will have been observed, and if the contracting parties sign the contract simultaneously in front of a notary or another competent official and two witnesses. An inheritance contract may be rescinded by the parties with a written agreement at any time.

Provisions applicable to the administration of the estate

Upon the death of the deceased, the estate in its entirety vests in the heirs. If the deceased did not appoint an executor, the heirs are jointly responsible for the administration and distribution of the estate. The heirs may apply for the appointment of a public estate administrator, or the competent authorities may appoint such an administrator if they deem it necessary to safeguard the estate and its correct distribution. If the deceased appointed an executor, the executor has sole possession of the assets of the estate, and has the power to manage, maintain and divide the estate.

Immediately after the demise of the testator, any testamentary provisions have to be filed with the competent authority, who must probate it and communicate the respective provisions to the heirs and legatees.

11.4 Trusts

No Swiss trust law

Anglo-saxon trust law has not been adopted into the Swiss legislation. There is no substantial Swiss law on trusts, and no such thing as a Swiss domestic trust. Therefore, a trust can only be established according to foreign law, whereby the settlor is free to choose the governing law. Despite the lack of substantial trust provisions, Swiss courts have been dealing with trusts for many years.

Recognition of foreign trusts

Switzerland is one of the largest trust administration centers in the world, and recognized the Hague Convention on the Law Applicable to Trusts and on their Recognition of 1 July 1985, which came into effect on 1 July 2007 (the Hague Convention — HTC), resulting in the recognition of trusts as a legal structure *sui generis,* and in the enforcement of foreign trusts.

55 art 511 para 1 CC

According to the HTC and the SPILA,[56] a trust shall be governed by the law chosen by the settlor. It is highly recommended to provide for such a choice of law rule in the trust deed, where the trust is closely connected to Switzerland (residence of trustee, location of assets, etc.), because if there is no choice of law rule, the trust shall be governed by the law to which the trust is most closely connected.[57] Again, under Swiss law there is no trust law and therefore the trust would not be recognized.

As trusts are recognized in Switzerland, a trustee can sue and be sued before Swiss courts in relation to the settlement of a trust, for example, in clawback claims brought by an heir in connection with a divorce and an estate under Swiss jurisdiction.

Preliminary issues related to the validity of wills or of other acts, by virtue of which assets are transferred to the trustee, are excluded from the scope of the Hague Convention, and consequently, from the law chosen by the parties in the trust deed.[58] Preliminary issues are governed by the law designated by the conflict of law rules of the respective forum. Hence, the acts by which property is transferred need to be valid under the law applicable to those transfers. The asset transfer into a trust may be invalid, for example, in case of incapacity of the settlor, non-fulfillment of the formal requirements, or invalidity of the underlying contract.

Swiss matrimonial property law and Swiss inheritance law (forced-heirship rules) contain provisions that have to be followed to ensure a valid and incontestable disposal of assets. These provisions in Swiss law cannot be derogated by voluntary acts.[59] The same is true for the provisions in Swiss law regarding creditor protection in matters of insolvency. As such, when setting up a trust the question whether heirs, husbands, wives, creditors, etc., can contest a contribution made to the trust, needs to be considered carefully.

While a testator may create a foundation by testamentary disposition or inheritance contract,[60] according to the prevailing doctrine, they may not create a testamentary trust under Swiss law. However, where a foreigner last domiciled in Switzerland has subjected his/her estate to the law of his/her citizenship, a trust may be set up by will, if the governing foreign law permits. While Swiss law generally allows the funding of an *inter vivos* trust by inheritance will, the compulsory portions of the statutory heirs of the settlor must be respected.

---

56 art 6 HTC and art 149c SPILA
57 art 7 HTC
58 art 4 HTC
59 art 15 HTC
60 art 81 para 1 CC

When acquiring real estate in Switzerland, the Lex Koller[61] has to be taken into consideration as well. While EU/EFTA nationals residing in Switzerland can acquire real estate without previous authorization, third-country nationals are still submitted to preliminary administrative authorization. If the trustee or the beneficiaries qualify as a person abroad the transfer is subject to authorization. In the case of a revocable trust, the settlor should be taken into consideration as well.

Taxation of trusts

The tax implications regarding trusts are not regulated by the Hague Convention. Accordingly, the Swiss Tax Conference issued Circular no. 30 in August 2007, with the intention of establishing a uniform practice throughout the different Swiss cantons. In 2008, the federal tax authorities declared Circular no. 30 as also being applicable to federal taxes.[62] Circular no. 30 provides guidelines for the cantonal authorities. As a non-legislative act, Circular no. 30 does not, however, establish any rights or obligations of the taxpayer.

According to Circular no. 30, a trust is not treated as a (foreign) law entity. The trust settlement is, therefore, generally disregarded and treated transparently for tax purposes. Consequently, the trust assets and the trust income will either be taxed by the settlor or the beneficiaries. Hence, a Swiss trustee is never assessed for taxation for the trust assets, nor for the trust income. While the trustee is regarded as the formal owner, he/she is not considered as the beneficial owner of the trust assets.

The taxation of trusts depends on the type of trust involved. One distinguishes between revocable, irrevocable, and discretionary trusts, and irrevocable fixed interest trusts.

For a trust to be irrevocable from a Swiss trust perspective, the trust deed must provide for it, and the settlor may not have the power to revoke the trust, neither as a beneficiary, nor due to having control of the facts, to decisively influence the trustee. In the case where the settlor retains a measure of control and has an economic benefit over the trust assets, the trust might qualify as a revocable trust (for tax purposes). The decision is subject to the discretion of the assessing tax authorities.

61 Federal Act on Acquisition of Property by Persons Domiciles Abroad of 16 December 1981, SR 211.412.41

62 Circular no. 20 of 27 March 2008

Circular no. 30 summarizes some basic principles of trust taxation for income and wealth tax purposes, but does not address inheritance and gift tax issues. The practice as outlined in Circular no. 20 of the Swiss Federal Tax Administration is generally binding to cantonal tax administrations. Nevertheless, the taxation of trust structures is a controversial issue in Switzerland, and therefore subject to detailed analysis on a case-by-case basis. As a result, it is recommended to request a tax ruling.

11.5 Reform movements

Inheritance law

In May 2013 the Federal Council announced the reform of the Swiss inheritance law and on 10 May 2017 it issued a press release on the ongoing reform project. The reform will modernize Swiss inheritance law, as the current law dates back to 1907. The first phase will focus on material changes, which in particular shall include the following.

The compulsory portion shall be reduced. The Federal Council suggests reducing the compulsory portion for children from $\frac{3}{4}$ to $\frac{1}{2}$ of the statutory share, and for the surviving spouse (registered partners respectively), from $\frac{1}{2}$ to $\frac{1}{4}$ of the statutory share. In case the deceased leaves children behind, the suggested changes therefore lead to the following compulsory portions:

Table 11.1 Compulsory portions

DECEASED LEAVES CHILDREN AND A SPOUSE	
Children today: $\frac{3}{8}$	after revision: $\frac{1}{4}$
Spouse today: $\frac{1}{4}$	after revision: $\frac{1}{8}$
Free disposable quota today: $\frac{3}{8}$	after revision: $\frac{5}{8}$

Where the deceased is not survived by anyone, the parent's current statutory entitlement shall be abolished. The proposed portions are, however, controversial, and will be reviewed again in the upcoming legislative procedure.

The expansion of the freely disposable quota favors business succession planning, as it avoids the fragmentation of companies. The drafted legislation includes further amendments designed to facilitate succession planning.

Cohabitants (unmarried couples/unregistered partners) who provided the deceased with substantial care and/or financial assistance shall be entitled to a certain amount of the estate if the deceased and the cohabitant have lived together in a joint household for at least three years, and the cohabitant would otherwise run into financial difficulties. The same shall apply to children who have lived in a common household with the deceased.

The second phase of the reform shall cover some technical aspects, such as the right to information.

Conflict of law rules on inheritance law

The international legal environment has changed, in particular due to the enactment of the EU SR. The Swiss conflict of law rules[63] shall be revised to enhance the compatibility of Swiss and foreign jurisdictions. The extension of the choice of law options shall allow a better coordination with foreign procedures, and provide for planning security. Therefore, anyone residing in Switzerland with a foreign nationality, shall have the option to declare the courts and authorities of his/her state of nationality to have jurisdiction over succession matters. With such a prorogation of jurisdiction, a competence conflict may be avoided. Furthermore, the Swiss conflict of law rules shall allow not only foreigners residing in Switzerland, but also Swiss dual citizens to opt that their foreign law of citizenship govern their estate. The further revision areas relate in particular to the applicable law on last wills and inheritance contracts, as well as to the recognition of foreign judgments, measurements, and documents.

Before relocating to Switzerland, individuals should familiarize themselves with Swiss matrimonial property law, rules relating to registered partners, and inheritance law. This chapter summarized the relevant legislation and issues that may have an impact on individuals' family affairs when moving to Switzerland.

63 art 86–96 SPILA

About the author

KINGA M. WEISS is a partner and co-chair of the private client team of Walder Wyss. Her areas of expertise are centered around both private clients and entrepreneurs in matters of succession law, including matrimonial property law related to estate planning, business succession, asset structuring, trust and endowment matters, as well as estate administration and litigation. Cross-border cases account for the bulk of her field of action. She is a member of the Expert Commission on the revision of the Swiss Private International Law Act on inheritance law. She regularly delivers speeches and publishes articles in and outside of Switzerland.

12 Schools

Rahel Bächtold, Rappold & Partner

State schools in Switzerland enjoy an excellent reputation. Approximately 96% of children in Switzerland attend state schools (in the canton of Zurich, this figure is approximately 94%).

State schools fulfill an important integrative function, as children and young people from different cultural, linguistic, and social backgrounds attend the same schools.

12.1 General

Attendance at state schools during the compulsory education period is free of charge. In state *Gymnasien* (upper-secondary baccalaureate schools), pupils must pay for the cost of educational materials. Childcare and supervision services (lunch, supervision before and after lessons) are also subject to cost.

Question: Which children can/must attend state school?

Answer: Assuming that they are of school age, all children registered and residing in Switzerland are entitled, and indeed obliged, to attend school. Nationality does not matter, and whether the parents are gainfully employed in Switzerland is of little importance. The determining factor is residence.

Question: Can a child also attend a Swiss school if the family is not resident in Switzerland?

Answer: In this case, only a private school can be considered. The Swiss Federation of Private Schools (*Verband Schweizer Privatschulen*; *swiss-schools.ch*) lists a large selection of private schools at all levels, from kindergarten to the *Gymnasium*.

Role and function of private schools in Switzerland

During the compulsory education period, a parent is permitted to remove his/her child from a state school and have him/her privately educated, provided that the chosen school is recognized by the state. Private schools are available in Switzerland at all levels, from kindergarten to the *Matura* qualification (general qualification for university entrance).

Private schools have different functions, for example:

- International schools
- Teaching in a different language
- Special educational concepts, for example, Rudolf Steiner or Montessori
- Religious upbringing
- Small classes to provide individual support, day-care facilities, etc.

12.2 Decentralized organization of state schools/federalist system

In Switzerland, each canton is primarily responsible for how its schools are organized; this includes learning content and learning aims. Consequently, the differing linguistic and cultural elements of the country (large city cantons, mountain regions, French, Romansch, and Italian Switzerland), can be better served.

It falls on the municipalities to implement cantonal stipulations and to take on the operational leadership of their schools. Municipalities also enjoy some leeway in deciding on specific arrangements.

Despite this variety of schools in Switzerland, pupils acquire comparable levels of knowledge over the course of their time at school. This is evident in the academic universities and *Fachhochschulen* (universities of applied sciences) attended by young adults from various cantons.

The Inter-cantonal Agreement on Harmonization of Compulsory Education (called the HarmoS Agreement) came into effect in August 2009. Its purpose is to standardize the compulsory education structure (eight years of primary level including preschool —

called kindergarten — as well as three years of lower-secondary education), and the start of compulsory schooling. Mandatory educational standards will also be implemented, as will collaboration in developing curricula and teaching materials. Not all cantons have joined the agreement; indeed, certain cantons have rejected membership through a cantonal referendum. That said, the majority of the cantons have submitted to the HarmoS Agreement. The following sections describe the organization and educational services of schools in those cantons that have joined HarmoS.

As the largest economic canton, Zurich and its school system will be presented near the end of the chapter in a separate section.

12.3 Starting school

The cut-off date for entry to kindergarten is 31 July, in accordance with the HarmoS Agreement. Children whose fourth birthday falls before this date can attend kindergarten the following autumn. Parents may submit individual requests for enrolment at an earlier or later date. The procedure is regulated.

Place of enrolment

Schools in Switzerland cannot be chosen freely; children are allocated a certain kindergarten or school according to their specific residential address. In principle, a child must attend the school that is assigned to that particular residential address. If need be, a petition can be filed for allocation to a different local school if there are sufficient grounds for doing so (usually on account of a dangerous or lengthy route to school).

12.4 Duration and breakdown of compulsory education

The compulsory schooling period is 11 years:
- Kindergarten (preschool): two years
- Primary school: six years
- Secondary school: three years (lower-secondary level)

Kindergarten

Kindergarten serves as preparation for school and is a blend of free play and guided lessons. There are no 'sets' (groupings of children based on performance). Particular value is attached to language development. In many cantons High German is therefore spoken, either in whole or in part, as early as kindergarten. Subject matter (numbers, letters) is not taught. Groups of approximately 18–22 children are supervized and led by a trained professional. Kindergarten teaching staff are up to 95.6% female.

Teaching time is not standardized; it can be set as pleased by the cantons and the municipalities. The cantons that have joined the HarmoS Agreement, however, are required to introduce core times, i.e. lessons throughout the morning as well as throughout the afternoon.

Primary school

As a rule, a child automatically enters primary school after two years of kindergarten, unless his/her development prevents this step from being taken. In this case, the second year at kindergarten is repeated. Conversely, it is possible to apply for early transition into primary school. The municipality regulates this process, and the wellbeing of the child is paramount. Applications for early enrolment and early transfer are only granted with the strictest caution. Upon moving to Switzerland, the fact that early enrolment is the norm in the pupil's country of origin or if the pupil has already attended kindergarten abroad, does not constitute sufficient grounds for an application.

Lessons take place in classes of mixed ability, and the teaching staff (predominantly female) are usually all-rounders.

Two languages are taught in addition to mathematics, history, civics, geography, science, art and design, practical crafts, music and sport. Switzerland has four recognized national languages (German, French, Italian and Romansch). This means that a second national language is taught at primary level, in addition to English. In German-speaking cantons, this is usually French. The HarmoS Agreement stipulates that English is taught in the third primary year at the latest, and that a second national language is taught in the fifth primary year at the latest. Many cantons, however, begin English lessons even earlier.

Secondary school (lower-secondary level)

Unlike primary school, specialist subject teachers teach at secondary level. This means that the children are taught by several different teachers in a range of different subjects.

Secondary schools in individual cantons are organized very differently; various lower-secondary models exist depending on the canton. Most cantons operate models in which pupils are assigned to lower or higher level classes according to their ability. A minority of cantons dispense with this kind of separation. In these cases, all pupils are taught in the same integrated model.

Lower-level pupils are not required to sit an examination when transitioning from primary level to lower-secondary level. Schools that place higher demands on pupils require recommendations from the primary level teachers. The pivotal factors are: a good academic performance, individual development, and working and learning behavior. In some cantons, pupils are required to pass an examination.

School hours and holidays up to lower-secondary level (as well as the *Gymnasium*)

The HarmoS Agreement stipulates that kindergarten and primary school hours should be organized into core times wherever possible. This means that the children, for example, attend kindergarten or primary school for one whole morning. Depending on the level, this is then followed by lessons in the afternoon; the number of lessons increases over the course of the compulsory schooling period.

Precise school hours are regulated by each canton and municipality, which is why no binding information can be given here. However, at primary level, lessons hardly ever begin before 8 am.

School holidays are also determined by the cantons and then by the municipalities within the cantons. The 'sport holidays' often vary within the same canton (out of consideration for the popular tourist regions), while the remaining holidays are usually regulated at cantonal level in a uniform manner. The following holiday model is widespread:

Sport holidays:	two weeks in the period end of January to beginning of March
Spring holidays:	two weeks in the period April to beginning of May
Summer holidays:	five weeks in the period July and August
Autumn holidays:	two weeks in the period end of September to end of October
Christmas holidays:	one to two weeks from Christmas to the beginning of January

Requests for children to miss some days of school may be submitted, but are only approved for very good reasons. To balance out the restrictive dispensation rules, many cantons recognize the 'joker day' system; amounting to one to three days off school per academic year, which can be chosen freely.

Extracurricular supervision

All-day school models do exist in Switzerland, but they are the exception rather than the rule. Extracurricular supervision is not regulated, but is left to (social) policy. Whether or not services are offered is therefore very diverse in Switzerland.

Broadly speaking, there is a good to very good range of childcare provision in big cities, although this is less/non existent in rural and village areas. In any event, enquiries must be made at each location.

Services offered by such institutions are roughly as follows:

- Lunch is often offered at the school itself or very close by, as is supervision before and after school hours, i.e. between 7 am and 6 pm. These services are not free of charge
- The staff are trained and provide professional childcare (free or guided play, crafts, gymnastics, homework support, group trips, etc.), and the children are required to integrate, and actively participate. Children from all social backgrounds attend these facilities and they are often made up of mixed age groups

Dealing with children with learning difficulties, mental disabilities, or physical disabilities at school

Over the last few years, Switzerland has experienced a change in attitude; many cantons stipulate that children with a mild physical or mental disability and children with learning difficulties should be integrated into regular lessons wherever possible. This is undertaken with the aid of trained special needs staff who support the class teacher and teach alongside them in some or all lessons. They take particular care of children with special needs. In a regular class, there are no more than one to three children with disabilities or children with learning difficulties. Many studies have shown that the experience is a positive one on both sides.

Special institutions are available for children with severe disabilities or children who cannot be integrated into regular schools. The school authorities allocate children to these institutions after a careful evaluation by specialists in consultation with the parents.

Governance, school management, and legal action

School governance is tiered and is usually administered by a board of laypersons who are democratically elected by members of the municipality. This board (often at the request of the school management) makes decisions about school policies (enrolment, skipping a year, repeating a year, moving into the class above, disciplinary measures, etc.). In smaller municipalities, participation on the school board is usually a secondary role outside the members' main jobs.

The canton assumes the overall supervision of schools. It makes educational policy decisions, carries out projects and school reforms, and passes the associated laws.

Purely operative leadership falls to each individual school management team; incidentally, this is not the case everywhere in Switzerland.

If parents do not agree with decisions about their children's schooling, legal options are available, although they are often time consuming and costly.

12.5 Post-compulsory education: upper-secondary level

90% of all young people continue their schooling after finishing their compulsory schooling, putting Switzerland at the forefront of OECD countries.

Post-compulsory education is divided into two main branches:

- Apprenticeships and *Berufsmaturität* — federal vocational baccalaureate (possibly specialized schools (*Fachmittelschule*) and specialized baccalaureate (*Fachmaturität*))
- Academic baccalaureate schools (*Maturitätsschule* (*Gymnasien*))

Academic baccalaureate schools and upper-secondary baccalaureate schools (*Gymnasium*)

In Switzerland, 20% of children attend an upper-secondary baccalaureate school (*Gymnasium*), which concludes with the *Matura* qualification (a school-leaving examination).

Each canton establishes the conditions for admission to the *Gymnasium*. Often, this is a combination of very good predicted grades and an examination. The first semester at the *Gymnasium* is considered a trial period. The actual *Gymnasium* education commences after compulsory education (at a *Kurzgymnasium* — a school lasting four years); in certain cantons, however, this may be even earlier (at a *Langzeitgymnasium* — a school lasting six years).[1] The *Matura* qualification entitles the student to enrol at universities, universities for teacher education and, following a vocational practical training program (*Berufspraktikum*), to universities for applied sciences. In Swiss universities only medical degree programs (medicine, dentistry, and veterinary medicine) and sport and exercise science are subject to admission restrictions (numerus clausus/aptitude test).

The express goal of the federally recognized academic baccalaureate schools (*Maturitätsschulen*) is to prepare pupils for the higher education entrance qualification. General education is paramount in the educational programs of these schools.

Pupils are taught seven compulsory subjects, one main specialization, and one secondary specialization:

- The compulsory subjects are: a first language (German, French, Italian, or Romansch), a second language (German, French, Italian), a third language (a third national language, English, or an ancient language), mathematics, science

1 The canton of Zurich offers the *Langzeitgymnasium* and the *Kurzzeitgymnasium*, see 12.7

(biology, chemistry, and physics), humanities and social sciences (history, geography, introduction to economics and law), visual arts, and/or music

- The main specialization is selected from the following eight subjects or subject groups: ancient languages (Latin and/or Greek), a modern language (a third national language, English, Spanish, or Russian), physics and applied mathematics, biology and chemistry, economics and law, philosophy/psychology/education, visual arts, music
- The secondary specialization is selected from the following 14 subjects or subject groups: physics, chemistry, biology, applied mathematics, IT, history, geography, philosophy, religious education, business and law, education/psychology, visual arts, music, sport

Owing to Switzerland's decentralized education system, and the extensive autonomy of the cantons, each canton's range of *Maturität* programs varies widely.

Question: Can my child, who previously attended an academic baccalaureate school, move to a Swiss *Gymnasium* without further action?

Answer: Each canton regulates its own conditions. As a rule, the following applies: if, in their home country, a pupil has previously attended a *Gymnasium*-style educational program and/or a school preparing pupils for university, and could continue to attend the same, he/she will be admitted to the *Gymnasium* for a trial semester without needing to sit an examination.

In any case, it is advisable to contact the desired *Gymnasium* in advance. When moving from Germany or Austria to German-speaking Switzerland, it must be noted that a high level of French is taught at the *Gymnasium*. If need be, individual learning aims can be agreed. It must also be noted that only 20% of young people in Switzerland attend a *Gymnasium*. Teaching standards and the demands placed on pupils are accordingly high.

Apprenticeship (Vocational Education and Training)[2]

One of the greatest strengths of the Swiss education system lies in apprenticeships. Apprenticeships are the largest and most important post-compulsory educational

---

2 see Educational Qualifications 200 Upper-Secondary and Tertiary Level p 23, *bfs.admin.ch*

route in Switzerland. Around 74% of young people opt for this route after compulsory education.[3] In Switzerland, Vocational Education and Training (VET — *Berufliche Grundbildung*) is organized according to the dual-track system. Practical training usually takes place at a training company; theoretical classes take place at a VET school. The VET school is attended one to one and a half days per week (those preparing for the Federal Vocational Baccalaureate (*Berufsmaturität*) attend on two days). Depending on the various professions, there may also be other obligatory specialized courses, which are organized by the professional associations. Around 10% of apprentices on VET programs learn their trade at a full-time vocational school (school and practical experience at the same company, or a placement following school education). This has greater significance in French-speaking Switzerland (25%) than in German-speaking Switzerland (4%).[4]

The basis of the VET scheme is the apprenticeship contract. The partners in this contract are the apprentice, and the vocational trainer (instructor). Training takes two to four years. The cantonal authority supervizes the VET route and is also responsible for administering the final examinations. It issues the VET diploma or the VET certificate upon successful completion of the course.[5]

The main educational fields among male students remain business and administration (18% of all vocational graduations), construction (16%), engineering and metalwork (10%), and vehicle/automobile (10%). Among female students, business and administration is at the top (33% of all vocational graduations), followed by trade (17%), and nursing and medical services (17%). Over the last 10 years, the number of VET graduations increased by 18%.[6]

An apprenticeship, as the training position at a company is called, must be sourced by the apprentices themselves. Companies select their apprentices based on their school grades, their application and also on the basis of an introductory interview. In the final school year of compulsory education, teachers provide skills training on how to apply for an apprenticeship. There are also many state support and advice services that young people can make use of free of charge.

In the last 20 years, the number of young people continuing their education after a basic apprenticeship program and achieving *Berufsmaturität* has been rising steadily. Graduating from an apprenticeship is no longer viewed merely as a goal, but as a stage in education.

3 Educational Qualifications 2010 Upper-Secondary and Tertiary Level p 23, *bfs.admin.ch*
4 Educational Qualifications 2010 Upper-Secondary and Tertiary Level p 23, *bfs.admin.ch*
5 Educational Qualifications 2010 Upper-Secondary and Tertiary Level p 23, *bfs.admin.ch*
6 Educational Qualifications 2010 Upper-Secondary and Tertiary Level p 23, *bfs.admin.ch*

Federal Vocational Baccalaureate (*Berufsmaturität*) schools

Federal Vocational Baccalaureate (*Berufsmaturität*) is defined as broader and deeper general education at upper-secondary level. It certifies that the holder has a higher education entrance qualification, i.e. entitles the holder to admission at a university of applied sciences, in a field of study that corresponds to the VET program. The holder does not need to sit an examination. Lessons are given to supplement on-the-job training and school education. Preparation can take place in two ways:[7]

- During the VET program (for three-year apprenticeships, usually from the first year; for four-year apprenticeships, sometimes from the second year) at a *Berufsmittelschule* with extended teaching (two days per week); or
- Subsequent to the VET program, by attending a corresponding educational institution for full- or part-time study (duration: two to three semesters)

The *Berufsmaturität* certificate is issued after passing a final examination (provided that the student also passes the final examination in the vocational and practical subjects).

Berufsmaturität tuition — entailing at least 1,440 lessons for the route completed during the VET program — encompasses the same six basic subjects for all channels:

- First national language
- Second national language
- Third language
- History/Political science
- Economics/Business studies/Law
- Mathematics

In addition, students study the channel-specific compulsory subjects and a secondary specialization.[8]

The *Berufsmaturität* is offered by around 200 schools: vocational secondary schools (*Berufsmittelschulen*), commercial business secondary schools (*Handelsmittelschulen*), apprenticeship workshops, and individual private schools.

Qualification entitles the holder to enrol at a university of applied sciences without needing to sit an examination. It is also possible to enrol at an academic university with further additional qualifications.

7 Educational Qualifications 2010 Upper-Secondary and Tertiary Level p 34, *bfs.admin.ch*

8 *Zugriff* January 2012, *bbt.admin.ch*

Specialized schools (*Fachmittelschule*) and the specialized baccalaureate (*Fachmaturität*)

The specialized school (*Fachmittelschule*) is a more recent institution in Switzerland. Following compulsory education, it provides a general education that leads to a specific occupational field. The *Fachmittelschule* lasts three years and prepares pupils for studies at a PET college (*Höhere Fachschule*) or a university of applied sciences (*Fachhochschule*).

Pupils are prepared for the following professional fields: health, social work, education, communications and IT, etc.

Further information on *Fachmittelschulen* and further professional prospects can be found at *berufsberatung.ch*.

The specialized baccalaureate (*Fachmaturität*) offers direct access to education at universities of applied sciences in the respective occupational fields. Those wishing to acquire the *Fachmaturität* must pass an additional one-year training module — usually practice-oriented — following their three-year education at a *Fachmittelschule*. They must also write a *Fachmaturität* essay.[9]

12.6 Tertiary level

Switzerland offers a wide range of attractive educational options at tertiary level. Depending on their vocational or general educational background, prospective students attend an institute of higher education (university, federal institute of technology, university of applied sciences, university of teacher education), or further training at tertiary level (at a *Höhere Fachschule* — PET college).

PET colleges (*Höhere Fachschulen*) and universities of applied sciences (*Fachhochschulen*)

The PET college (*Höhere Fachschule*) is a Swiss particularity, seen less frequently in other countries. It offers training programs at tertiary level beyond the university field, for more demanding occupational fields and leadership positions. It also offers management training and helps those who have completed a three- to four-year VET program to specialize.[10] Unlike universities of applied sciences (*Fachhochschulen*) (see next section), PET colleges focus on a narrower subject

9 Educational Qualifications 2010 Upper-Secondary and Tertiary Level p 33, *bfs.admin.ch*
10 *educa.ch*

area and are less academic. As a rule, the graduates of these pathways are younger than those sitting a federal examination. Training often commences directly after graduating upper-secondary level, or within three or four years thereof, and serves as a foundation for a professional career.[11] The *Konferenz der Höheren Fachschulen* website provides a list of all *Fachschulen* in Switzerland at *konferenz-hf.ch.*

Fachhochschulen offer practice-oriented and application-oriented degree programs that lead to professional qualifications at bachelor level, like academic universities. Since 2008, *Fachhochschulen* have provided additional in-depth, specialized and research-based content at master's level to prepare students for an advanced professional qualification. The master's course takes one to one and a half years. In total, there are seven regional state *Fachhochschulen* and two recognized private *Fachhochschulen.*[12] As with academic universities, the Bologna System applies: ECTS points are awarded.

Academic universities and Swiss Federal Institutes of Technology

In Switzerland there are 12 recognized universities as well as two Swiss Federal Institutes of Technology (in Zurich and Lausanne). Further information about the various universities can be found at *educa.ch.*

Traditional academic universities (*Universitäre Hochschulen* — UH) are funded by the state. Switzerland also has a range of private universities and institutions that offer courses and qualifications; however, these are largely not recognized and are difficult to classify adequately in the country's education system. Until now, a small number of private higher education institutions, or study programs delivered by private higher education facilities, have been accredited by the Swiss University Conference (SUK).[13]

12.7 Schools in the canton of Zurich

The canton of Zurich is a member of the HarmoS Agreement. Therefore, a total of 11 years of compulsory education applies; two years of kindergarten level, six years of primary level, and three years of secondary level. Kindergarten forms part of the cantonal Volksschule system (primary and lower-secondary education combined).

11 Educational Qualifications 2010 Upper-Secondary and Tertiary Level p 50, *bfs.admin.ch*
12 *educa.ch*
13 *educa.ch*

Organization

The canton of Zurich encompasses 171 municipalities, in which the cities (Zurich, Winterthur, Uster, Effretikon) are legally also municipalities. The municipal school board (i.e. people elected by the populace, often as a secondary office, mainly in smaller municipalities) is responsible for all individual decisions concerning a school's policy. The school board usually encompasses a presiding committee and, depending on the size of the community, 5–30 board members.

Enrolment

The cut-off date for enrolment is currently 30 April. Children who turn four before 30 April join kindergarten, i.e. are enrolled, after the summer holidays (mid/end August). The cut-off date is gradually being pushed back to 31 July by 2020 (HarmoS Agreement).[14] Children who are already four years old by 31 July can be admitted at the parents' request.

Younger children can only be enrolled early for very good reasons and only upon successful application. Delaying a child's enrolment is only possible if the expected difficulties cannot be met with special educational measures. In both cases (early or late enrolment), parents must file an application to the school board of the municipality where they live.

School year/holidays

One school year lasts from mid August to the start of July (in the canton of Zurich, school starts on the Monday of the 34th calendar week). Autumn, Christmas, sport, spring, and summer holidays (totaling 13 weeks) are scheduled in between, which reduces effective school time to 39 calendar weeks. These regulations also apply to *Gymnasium* schools in the canton of Zurich.

School hours

At all levels, teaching time or supervision lasts from 8 am to 12 pm (core times); it is possible to reduce these hours by 20 minutes, for example, by starting lessons at 8.20 am, for organizational reasons. In the afternoons, it is up to the municipalities to offer core times or individual lesson times. With the exception of the *Gymnasium*, there is no school on Wednesday afternoons throughout all 11 years.

14 The cut-off days for enrolment are: 30 June in the 2017/2018 school year; and 15 July in the 2018/2019 school year

Absences and joker days

Children must participate in lessons and can only be excused from lessons in certain exceptional cases. The parents must make the relevant petition to the school. The school offers two joker days per school year at all levels.

Special educational measures/supporting gifted pupils

Children with learning difficulties or behavioral issues are integrated into normal classes wherever possible, and are encouraged and supported with the use of specific measures. Special educational measures include speech therapy, German as a Foreign Language, painting and dance therapy, supporting gifted pupils, psychomotricity, etc.

Should special educational measures be necessary, teaching staff and parents will decide the appropriate steps in discussion with one another.

Music schools

The larger municipalities run fee-based music schools which can be attended voluntarily.

Supporting services

The *Volkschule* is obliged to look after the health of its children. Regular visits from the school doctor and school dentist examine all children of schoolgoing age. Parents can excuse their children from these visits.

Educational psychology services and school social services complement and support the work of the teaching staff.

Private kindergartens and private schools

On request, the entire compulsory education period can be completed at a private school. Private schools charge varying fees that must be covered fully by the parents. It is best to enquire directly with the kindergarten/school in question regarding its services and costs. Private kindergartens and schools require an operating licence from the canton of Zurich in order to recognize their educational offering.

Supervision outside of school hours

Supervision or childcare services outside of school hours, i.e. during lunch or in the afternoon, do not need to be organized by the school. The municipalities are, however, obliged to determine the need for extracurricular supervision, and provide the corresponding services (lunch, crèche, all-day schools, or student clubs). These supervized services are subject to charge — the amount usually depends on the parents' income.

Despite this legal obligation among the municipalities, there is still a lack of facilities for extracurricular supervision in many places. Even in the city of Zurich, crèches are in short supply.

The *Gymnasium*

In the canton of Zurich, a pupil may transfer to a *Gymnasium* if he/she has good grades and has passed an examination after the sixth year of primary school, or the second or third year of secondary school. Starting after the sixth year of primary school, a *Gymnasium* education takes six years (a *Langzeitgymnasium*). Starting after the second or third year of secondary school, a *Gymnasium* education takes four years (a *Kurzzeitgymnasium*).

There are five different *Maturität* profiles:[15]

- Ancient languages profile (language combination contains Latin and/or Greek, and main specialization is a language)
- Modern languages profile (language combination contains only modern languages and the main specialization is a language)
- Mathematics-Science profile (main specialization is biology and chemistry or physics and applied mathematics)
- Economics-Law profile (main specialization is economics and law)
- Music profile (main specialization is visual arts or music)

The *Maturität* profile must be selected at the start of the 11th school year.

In addition, there is the *Liceo Artistico*, which meets both Swiss and Italian *Maturität* requirements as an academic secondary school specializing in visual arts. It is co-managed by Switzerland and Italy.

For musically gifted pupils, or those particularly talented in sports, special classes are offered at individual *Gymnasium* schools. Some classes also deliver all teaching content in English.

15 *mba.ch*

12.8 International comparison/PISA study

The international benchmarking of educational systems is gaining increasing significance. Studies such as the OECD's Program for International Student Assessment (PISA) enable the Swiss educational system to be ranked internationally. This means that the skills of 15-year-old pupils are compared internationally.

The results from the latest PISA study of 2009 made it abundantly clear that young people in Switzerland have attained good knowledge and skills by the end of their compulsory education. In all test areas of PISA — reading, mathematics, science, and problem-solving — Swiss pupils achieved results above the OECD average. The national averages in problem-solving and science are significantly higher.[16]

Switzerland offers an excellent education system with a variety of schooling options available. This chapter provided an overview of the different types of schools, universities, and other educational institutions across all cantons.

Links to useful online resources

- *educa.ch*
  The Swiss Education Server (SBS) offers access to all relevant information regarding the Swiss education system, and is the official platform for cantonal, inter-cantonal and Swiss-wide educational institutes. The website provides a structured overview of information and resources from schools, universities of teacher education, vocational training and adult education institutions, as well as teaching subject vacancies
- *berufsberatung.ch*
  This is the most comprehensive database in Switzerland, with continuing education services in the non-university field. As a joint project by the Swiss Confederation and the cantons, it contains over 30,000 courses and apprenticeships, considers all areas of continuing education, covers all linguistic regions, and provides a transparent view of continuing education services across Switzerland. The site is quality assured and continually updated

16 *pisa2009.ch*

- *edk.ch*
  The Swiss Conference of Cantonal Ministers of Education (EDK) is a political body of 26 cantonal ministers of education responsible for teaching, education, culture, and sport. The EDK is responsible for national coordination in all fields of education and cultural policy. The website offers a good overview of the Swiss education system
- *bbt.admin.ch*
  The Swiss Federal Office for Professional Education and Technology (BBT) is the Confederation's centre of excellence for issues on vocational training, universities of applied sciences, and promoting innovation. The website is very comprehensive and displays current developments
- *swiss-schools.ch*
  The Federation of Swiss Private Schools (VSP) has around 260 schools, including the most significant and oldest in the country. Approximately 100,000 pupils from over 100 countries attend a private school in Switzerland. It is very easy to find a suitable school on the website
- *edu.ch*
  This website is a private platform for links on the topic of schools, with a focus on Switzerland

About the author

RAHEL BÄCHTOLD was born in 1965 and raised in Schaffhausen, Switzerland. She obtained a degree in law from the University of Zurich in 1989 and was admitted to the Bar in 1993. Since 1994, Rachel has been partner at Zurich-based law firm Rappold & Partner. She specializes in employment law and education law.

13 Swiss Citizenship[1]

Dr. Christian H. Kälin, Henley & Partners

Following an extensive political debate about a much-needed reform of the Swiss Citizenship Act (SCA), a new revised SCA was approved by the Swiss parliament on 20 June 2014 (nSCA). This became law on 1 January 2018.

13.1 Regular acquisition of citizenship: *ius sanguinis*

The *ius sanguinis,* or bloodline citizenship, remains the decisive legal principle for the acquisition of Swiss citizenship. This can be explained not least by the fact that Switzerland, like Luxembourg, for example, has had an unusually high proportion of people born outside its territory for years, many of whom are active within international organizations or multinational companies, and thus contribute indirectly to the country's domestic prosperity.[2] Art 1 of the nSCA applies. According to the nSCA, the legitimate child of a Swiss national acquires Swiss citizenship at birth.[3] Likewise, the illegitimate child of a Swiss citizen acquires Swiss citizenship at birth if the mother is a Swiss citizen, or otherwise, if he/she had already acquired citizenship at birth upon the presentation of a declaration of paternity to the relevant authority.[4] This also applies to adoption cases.[5] Accordingly, a minor acquires the cantonal and communal citizenship of the adopter, and thus Swiss citizenship when he/she is adopted by a Swiss citizen.

1 Adapted from the chapter on Swiss citizenship in Kälin, *Ius Doni: The Acquisition of Citizenship by Investment* (2016)
2 Joppke (2012)
3 art 1(1) nSCA
4 art 1(2) nSCA
5 art 4 nSCA

13.2 Combination of citizenship of the municipality and canton

Swiss citizenship is acquired on the basis of possessing a cantonal citizenship which, in turn, is based on citizenship in a particular municipality, and is distinctly directly democratic in form.[6]

A child acquires the cantonal and municipal citizenship and 'Place of Origin'[7] of his/her parents, which emphasizes the origin principle as the dominant principle underpinning citizenship in Switzerland. Instead of place of birth, the Swiss passport has a 'Place of Origin' field, which lists the commune(s) and canton(s) of which the holder is a citizen. It is possible to hold multiple citizenships within Switzerland, i.e. holding citizenship in more than one municipality and more than one canton.

The pronouncedly federal and directly democratic constitution of Switzerland is slightly moderated, in that the legal minimal requirements for the acquisition and loss of Swiss citizenship are regulated by the Swiss Federal State.[8] Also, the Swiss Federal State ultimately grants naturalization on federal level and thus has the final say.[9] Nevertheless, both the federal and the directly democratic structure in Switzerland find expression here, in that the Swiss State may only provide minimum requirements for the naturalization of foreigners by the cantons.[10] Given that federal law only sets minimum requirements, the cantons and municipalities retain considerable regulatory scope, which is expressed in the diversity of administrative procedures, forms, and conditions provided for naturalization,[11] although this has been somewhat streamlined in the nSCA. This diversity, as often happens in Switzerland, results in quite significant administrative duplication.[12] The Swiss Federal State grants Swiss citizenship within a framework of 'simplified naturalization', which concerns mainly applications on the basis of marriage to a Swiss citizen, after prior consultation at all three levels — federal, cantonal, and municipal. Jointly, the latter two levels are primarily involved in 'regular naturalization',[13] meaning that an applicant's access to Swiss citizenship most often falls at the hurdles on cantonal, and in particular municipal level, as far

6 Jackson in Aleinikoff, Klusmeyer (2001)
7 *'Heimatort'*
8 art 38(1)(1) SCst
9 art 38(2) SCst
10 In accordance with art 15(a) ChBüG, the naturalization process is regulated, in contrast to the definition of the substantive criteria for naturalization by cantonal law
11 D'Amato in d'Amato, Gerber (2005)
12 Steiner, Wicker (2004); Uslucan (2012)
13 under art 38 SCst

more applications are rejected by the municipalities than by the cantonal or the federal authorities, respectively.[14]

13.3 Acquisition of Swiss citizenship by naturalization

While the Swiss Federal State provides the overall framework,[15] the cantons are in fact responsible for the actual naturalization of foreign persons.[16] However, the federal authorities must still give the final consent.[17] The provisions regarding regular naturalization are contained in arts 9 to 18 of the nSCA.

The nSCA requires that the applicant must hold a permanent residence permit, and must have resided in Switzerland for at least 10 years, of which three must have been spent in Switzerland within the last five years before applying for naturalization.[18] The time spent in Switzerland between the applicant's eighth and 18th birthdays are now counted double.[19] However, the effective period of residence must in any case be six years.[20]

It also requires that the applicant has to be integrated into Swiss society and not pose a threat to public security.[21]

Additionally, cantons and municipalities may provide for further, additional requirements, for example, knowledge of the local language, or additional residence requirements in the relevant canton or municipality.[22] The new law, however, requires cantons to provide conditions within a certain framework, for example, to provide for a minimum residence requirement of two to five years.[23]

The relatively strict naturalization provisions undergo some mitigation in the case of so-called 'simplified naturalization'. The nSCA differentiates between regular and simplified naturalizations;[24] simplified naturalizations principally concern spouses of Swiss citizens, as well as a few special cases.

The simplified naturalization process requires that the applicant is integrated into Switzerland,[25] does not pose a threat to the internal or external security of

14 Hainmueller, Hangartner (2013) p 160 re the autonomy of municipalities; Uslucan (2012) and Schönberger (2005) p 90
15 art 38(1) SCst
16 art 38(2) SCst
17 art 12(2) SCA, art 9 nSCA
18 art 9 nSCA
19 art 9(2) nSCA
20 art 9(2) nSCA
21 art 11 nSCA
22 This is specifically provided for in art 12(3) nSCA
23 art 18(1) nSCA
24 art 20 nSCA
25 art 20(1) nSCA

Switzerland,[26] after marrying a Swiss citizen, he/she may apply for naturalization, having lived in Switzerland for a total of five years (and having lived in Switzerland for the whole previous year),[27] and having lived in marital union with a Swiss citizen for three years.[28] Considered together, this means that foreign spouses will acquire Swiss citizenship after three years of marriage and five years of residence, benefiting them and their children. In terms of their legal nature, Swiss simplified naturalization acts are considered as justiciable legal applications that must meet the requirements of the Federal Constitution.[29] They cannot be subject to direct democratic votes and are exclusively subject to written statutory law. They can be challenged in cantonal courts and be annulled following a constitutional appeal before the Federal Court.

13.4 Suitability for naturalization

In material terms, the central conditions for the granting of Swiss citizenship are provided by art 11 of the nSCA and art 12 of the nSCA, which state that it is necessary to determine whether an applicant is qualified for naturalization before granting authorization.[30] As emphasized by the wording of art 11 and 12 of the nSCA in particular, the suitability criteria are not exhaustive, but allow the granting authority a considerable margin of discretion based on the facts. Whether naturalization is granted is decided on according to whether the applicant is successfully 'integrated' into Swiss society,[31] is familiar with the Swiss way of life,[32] and does not pose a threat to the internal and external security of Switzerland.[33] Art 12 of the nSCA further clarifies these points and requests that the applicant must, at all times, have respected the public order and security[34] and the Swiss constitution,[35] have the ability to communicate in one of the national languages,[36]

26 art 20(2) nSCA
27 art 21(1)(b) nSCA
28 art 21(1)(a) nSCA
29 Abderhalden, Ehrenzeller (2008); Hainmueller, Hangartner (2013) pp 160 and 162
30 For greater detail on the historic criteria for integration in Switzerland: Argast (2007), which largely continues to apply in principle in the Swiss naturalization rules even under the nSCA. In this regard, also Caroni, Grasdorf-Meyer, Ott, Scheiber (2014)
31 art 11(a) nSCA
32 art 11(b) nSCA
33 art 11(c) nSCA
34 art 12(1)(a) nSCA
35 art 12(1)(b) nSCA
36 art 12(1)(c) nSCA

participate in economic activity, or acquire skills through education,[37] and assist in the integration of the spouse and/or the children of which the applicant has custody.[38] The presupposed integration of the applicant under art 11(a) nSCA requires good language skills and knowledge of culture and history, which can be determined in part by a written aptitude test. Various forms of such tests are the norm in the citizenship application procedures in Switzerland. These provisions are thus a prime example of final point theory citizenship legislation; the applicant who wishes to become a Swiss citizen has to show that he/she is already largely integrated into Swiss society.

The applicant's country of origin is furthermore, not by law of course, but effectively in practice, a decisive factor in a successful application for naturalization in Switzerland.[39] Switzerland does not, however, have provisions in its citizenship law that come even close to incorporating *ius doni* (citizenship-by-investment) principles.

This chapter provided a brief overview of the requirements for Swiss naturalization (regular and simplified) and citizenship.

37 art 12(1)(d) nSCA
38 art 12(1)(e) nSCA
39 Hainmueller, Hangartner (2013) p 185

About the author

DR. CHRISTIAN H. KÄLIN, TEP, IMCM, Chairman of Henley & Partners, is considered one of the world's foremost experts in investment migration and citizenship-by-investment, a field he pioneered. Holding master's and PhD degrees in law from the University of Zurich, he is a sought-after speaker and advises governments and international organizations. He is the author, co-author, or editor of many publications, including standard works such as the *Global Residence and Citizenship Handbook*, the *Henley & Partners – Kochenov Quality of Nationality Index*, and the *Switzerland Business & Investment Handbook*.

www.ingramcontent.com/pod-product-compliance
Lightning Source LLC
Chambersburg PA
CBHW071332230926
51849CB00002B/373

* 9 7 8 3 9 5 2 3 8 5 9 7 5 *